M783.342 Modern 1904 v. 2
Modern French songs :

THE MUSICIANS LIBRARY
FIFTY VOLUMES ISSUED

Song Volumes

JOHANNES BRAHMS: FORTY SONGS
High Voice. Low Voice
Edited by James Huneker

ROBERT FRANZ: FIFTY SONGS
High Voice. Low Voice
Edited by William Foster Apthorp

EDVARD GRIEG: FIFTY SONGS
High Voice. Low Voice
Edited by Henry T. Finck

GEORGE FRIDERIC HANDEL
VOL. I. SONGS AND AIRS FOR HIGH VOICE
VOL. II. SONGS AND AIRS FOR LOW VOICE
Edited by Ebenezer Prout

FRANZ SCHUBERT: FIFTY SONGS
High Voice. Low Voice
Edited by Henry T. Finck

ROBERT SCHUMANN: FIFTY SONGS
High Voice. Low Voice
Edited by W. J. Henderson

RICHARD WAGNER: LYRICS FOR SOPRANO
Edited by Carl Armbruster

RICHARD WAGNER: LYRICS FOR TENOR
Edited by Carl Armbruster

RICHARD WAGNER
LYRICS FOR BARITONE AND BASS
Edited by Carl Armbruster

HUGO WOLF: FIFTY SONGS
High Voice
Edited by Ernest Newman

. .

FIFTY MASTERSONGS
High Voice. Low Voice
Edited by Henry T. Finck

FIFTY SHAKSPERE SONGS
High Voice. Low Voice
Edited by Charles Vincent

MODERN FRENCH SONGS
High Voice. Low Voice
VOL. I. BEMBERG TO FRANCK
VOL. II. GEORGES TO WIDOR
Edited by Philip Hale

SEVENTY SCOTTISH SONGS
High Voice. Low Voice
Edited, with accompaniments, by Helen Hopekirk

SONGS BY THIRTY AMERICANS
High Voice. Low Voice
Edited by Rupert Hughes

SONGS FROM THE OPERAS FOR SOPRANO
Edited by H. E. Krehbiel

SONGS FROM THE OPERAS FOR MEZZO SOPRANO
Edited by H. E. Krehbiel

SONGS FROM THE OPERAS FOR ALTO
Edited by H. E. Krehbiel

Piano Volumes

JOHANN SEBASTIAN BACH
VOL. I. SHORTER PIANO COMPOSITIONS
VOL. II. LARGER PIANO COMPOSITIONS
Edited by Ebenezer Prout

LUDWIG VAN BEETHOVEN
VOLS. I & II. PIANO COMPOSITIONS
Edited by Eugen d'Albert

FRÉDÉRIC CHOPIN: FORTY PIANO COMPOSITIONS
Edited by James Huneker

FRÉDÉRIC CHOPIN: THE GREATER CHOPIN
Edited by James Huneker

S. COLERIDGE-TAYLOR
TWENTY-FOUR NEGRO MELODIES
Transcribed for the piano

EDVARD GRIEG: LARGER PIANO COMPOSITIONS
Edited by Bertha Feiring Tapper

FRANZ JOSEPH HAYDN: TWENTY PIANO COMPOSITIONS
Edited by Xaver Scharwenka

FRANZ LISZT: TWENTY ORIGINAL PIANO COMPOSITIONS
Edited by August Spanuth

FRANZ LISZT: TWENTY PIANO TRANSCRIPTIONS
Edited by August Spanuth

FRANZ LISZT: TEN HUNGARIAN RHAPSODIES
Edited by August Spanuth and John Orth

FELIX MENDELSSOHN: THIRTY PIANO COMPOSITIONS
Edited by Percy Goetschius

WOLFGANG AMADEUS MOZART
TWENTY PIANO COMPOSITIONS
Edited by Carl Reinecke

ROBERT SCHUMANN: FIFTY PIANO COMPOSITIONS
Edited by Xaver Scharwenka

RICHARD WAGNER
SELECTIONS FROM THE MUSIC DRAMAS
Arranged for the piano by Otto Singer

. .

ANTHOLOGY OF FRENCH PIANO MUSIC
VOL. I. EARLY COMPOSERS
VOL. II. MODERN COMPOSERS
Edited by Isidor Philipp

EARLY ITALIAN PIANO MUSIC
Edited by M. Esposito

Price of each volume, paper, cloth back, $1.50; full cloth, gilt, $2.50. Prices include postage.

MODERN FRENCH SONGS
VOLUME II

CONTENTS

	PAGE
THOMAS, AMBROISE (1811–1896)	
Evening (*Le Soir*)	134
THOMÉ, FRANCIS (1850–)	
A Love Sonnet (*Sonnet d'amour*)	138
WIDOR, CHARLES M. (1845–)	
The Sigh (*Soupir*)	140

INDEX

[ENGLISH]

	COMPOSER	VOL.	PAGE
Bell, The	Saint-Saëns	II	124
Bells, The	Debussy	I	65
Bygone Days	Delibes	I	99
Captive, The	Lalo	II	68
Clouds, The	Bouval	I	32
Come and embark	Godard	II	8
Could I forget?	Chrétien	I	56
Could my songs, their way be winging	Hahn	II	41
Countess, in thy dancing	Lemaire	II	71
Cradles, The	Fauré	I	117
Dead, The	Chausson	I	52
Death of Lovers, The	Debussy	I	81
Ecstasy	Duparc	I	105
Evening	Thomas	II	134
Evening Harmony	Debussy	I	74
Ferret, The	Bréville	I	38
Flower Message, A	Bouval	I	28
Gathered Rose, The	Franck	I	141
Gavotte of the Masquerade	Georges	II	1
Good morning, Claire!	Pessard	II	104
Haï Luli	Coquard	I	60
Havanaise	Paladilhe	II	94
Hindoo Song	Bemberg	I	1
How brief is the hour	Massenet	II	92
If thou shouldst tell me	Chaminade	I	48
In the Woods	Bizet	I	13
Irish Noël, An	Holmès	II	49
I've such a host of things to tell you	Ferrari	I	126
Love	Godard	II	13
Love Sonnet, A	Thomé	II	138
Lullaby	Ropartz	II	115
Madrigal	d'Indy	II	58
Maids of Cadiz, The	Delibes	I	91
Marriage of Roses	Franck	I	135
Medjé	Gounod	II	23
Memories of Yore	Hüe	II	53
Moonlight	Fauré	I	112
Moonlight	Saint-Saëns	II	130
Nile, The	Leroux	II	77
Open thy blue eyes	Massenet	II	88
Pastoral	Bizet	I	19
Perfect Hour, The	Hahn	II	38
Perfume of a Flower	Blanc	I	24
Provence Song	Massenet	II	84
Remembrance	Godard	II	5
Romance	Debussy	I	85
Roses of Ispahan, The	Fauré	I	121

[FRENCH]

	COMPOSER	VOL.	PAGE
Amour, L'	Godard	II	13
Au Printemps	Gounod	II	17
Berceaux, Les	Fauré	I	117
Berceuse	Ropartz	II	115
Bonjour, Suzon!	Pessard	II	104
Brises d'autrefois	Hüe	II	53
Chant Hindou	Bemberg	I	1
Chant Provençal	Massenet	II	84
Clair de lune	Fauré	I	112
Clair de lune	Saint-Saëns	II	130
Cloche, La	Saint-Saëns	II	124
Cloches, Les	Debussy	I	65
Embarquez-vous!	Godard	II	8
Esclave, L'	Lalo	II	68
Extase	Duparc	I	105
Filles de Cadix, Les	Delibes	I	91
Fleur messagère	Bouval	I	28
Furet du bois joli, Le	Bréville	I	38
Gavotte du Masque	Georges	II	1
Haï Luli	Coquard	I	60
Harmonie du Soir	Debussy	I	74
Havanaise	Paladilhe	II	94
Heure exquise, L'	Hahn	II	38
Il pleure dans mon cœur	Debussy	I	68
J'ai tant de choses à vous dire	Ferrari	I	126
Jours passés	Delibes	I	99
Lied	Franck	I	141
Lied maritime	d'Indy	II	62
Madrigal	d'Indy	II	58
Mariage des roses, Le	Franck	I	135
Medjé	Gounod	II	23
Mort des amants, La	Debussy	I	81
Morts, Les	Chausson	I	52
Nil, Le	Leroux	II	77
Noël d'Irlande	Holmès	II	49
Nuages, Les	Bouval	I	32
Ombre des arbres, L'	Debussy	I	88
Ouvre tes yeux bleus	Massenet	II	88
Parfum de fleur	Blanc	I	24
Pastorale	Bizet	I	19
Que je t'oublie?	Chrétien	I	56
Que l'heure est donc brève	Massenet	II	92
Romance	Debussy	I	85
Roses d'hiver, Les	Fontenailles	I	130
Roses d'Ispahan, Les	Fauré	I	121
Sérénade	Pierné	II	109
Si j'étais jardinier	Chaminade	I	43
Si mes vers avaient des ailes!	Hahn	II	41
Si vous n'avez rien à me dire	Rothschild	II	120

INDEX

[ENGLISH]

	COMPOSER	VOL.	PAGE
Sea Song, A	d'Indy	II	62
Serenade	Pierné	II	109
Shadow of Trees, The	Debussy	I	88
Sigh, A	Duparc	I	108
Sigh, The	Widor	II	140
Tears fall in my soul, The	Debussy	I	68
Threnody, A	Holmès	II	44
To Spring	Gounod	II	17
Valley, The	Gounod	II	31
Villanelle	Berlioz	I	7
Were I gardener	Chaminade	I	43
Why with your lovely presence haunt me	Rothschild	II	120
Winter Roses	Fontenailles	I	130

[FRENCH]

	COMPOSER	VOL.	PAGE
Soir, Le	Thomas	II	134
Sonnet d'amour	Thomé	II	138
Soupir	Duparc	I	108
Soupir	Widor	II	140
Te souviens-tu?	Godard	II	5
Thrînôdia	Holmès	II	44
Tu me dirais	Chaminade	I	48
Vallon, Le	Gounod	II	31
Vieille Chanson	Bizet	I	13
Villanelle	Berlioz	I	7
Vous dansez, Marquise	Lemaire	II	71

JULES MASSENET

CHARLES GOUNOD

CAMILLE SAINT-SAËNS

ÉDOUARD LALO

AUGUSTA HOLMÈS

BENJAMIN GODARD

VINCENT D'INDY

ALEXANDRE GEORGES

GEORGES HÜE

MODERN FRENCH SONGS

BIOGRAPHICAL SKETCHES

GREATER attention has been paid in the preparation of these sketches to the ultra-modern composers, or to those comparatively unknown in this country, than to those whose lives are recorded at length in English music dictionaries. An exception has been made in the case of Berlioz, Massenet and Saint-Saëns, with a view to the dates of compositions.

The reader will find much information concerning the operas, oratorios and cantatas of composers here mentioned by consulting Adolphe Jullien's "Musiciens d'Aujourd'hui," 2 vols. (Paris, 1892–94). Other books of reference are the *Mercure de France* (published in Paris monthly), the volumes of collected *feuilletons* by "Willy," or "L'Ouvreuse" — Henri Gauthier-Villars (1890–1901); and Gustave Robert's "La Musique à Paris" (1894–1900).

When the name of a city is not mentioned in connection with the performance of an opera or other work, the town of that performance was Paris.

ABBREVIATIONS: *a.*—act; *acc.*—accompaniment; *cant.*—cantata; *comp.*—composed; *dr. leg.*—dramatic legend; *dr. or.*—dramatic oratorio; *dr. sc.*—dramatic scene; *dr. sym.*—dramatic symphony; *fant.*—fantasia; *in coll.*—in collaboration; *lyr. com.*—lyric comedy; *lyr. dr.*—lyric drama; *lyr. ep.*—lyric episode; *lyr. pant.*—lyric pantomime; *lyr. sc.*—lyric scene; *lyr. sym.*—lyric symphony; *lyr. tr.*—lyric tragedy; *mus. com.*—musical comedy; *m. d.*—music drama; *mim.*—mimodrama; *op.*—grand opera; *Opé.*—the Paris Opéra; *op. c.*—opéra-comique; *Op. C.*—the theatre of the Opéra Comique, Paris; *or.*—oratorio; *ov.*—overture; *pant.*—pantomime; *perf.*—performed; *sc.*—scena; *son.*—sonata; *sym.*—symphony; *sym. p.*—symphonic poem.

GEORGES, ALEXANDRE
Born at Arras, February 25, 1850. Pupil at the Ecole Niedermeyer, Paris, where he took prizes. Organist of St. Vincent de Paul and teacher at the Ecole Niedermeyer. "Le Printemps," *op. c.* 1 *a.* (Paris, 1888); "Poèmes d'Amour," *lyr. op.* 3 *a.* (Paris, 1892); "Charlotte Corday," *lyr. dr.* 3 *a.* (1901); incidental music for Villiers de l'Isle-Adam's "Nouveau Monde" (1883) and "Axel" (1894); for "Alceste" (1891). "Nôtre Dame de Lourdes," *or.* (1899); "Le Chemin de Croix," *or.*; "Naissance de Venus," *sym. p.* (1898); music to the "Passion;" "Danses Chantées;" "Chansons de Miarka" (1895); songs, etc.

GODARD, BENJAMIN
Born at Paris, August 18, 1849; died at Cannes, January 11, 1895. Pupil of Richard Hammer and Vieuxtemp; pupil of Reber (composition) at Paris Conservatory, he competed in vain for the prix de Rome, 1866–67. Violinist, quartet player (viola) and conductor. He was awarded the Prix Chartier by the Institute of France for "merit shown in the department of chamber-music."

Operas: "Pedro de Zalema," *op.* 4 *a.* (Antwerp, 1884); "Jocelyn," *op.* 4 *a.* (Brussels, 1888); "Dante," *lyr. dr.* 4 *a.* (1890); "La Vivandière," *op. c.*—orchestration completed by Paul Vidal (1895); "Les Guelfes," *op.* 5 *a.*—overture played in 1883—(Rouen, 1902).

Stage music to Legendre's "Beaucoup de bruit pour rien," after Shakespeare (1887); to Fabre's "Jeanne d'Arc" (1891).

Orchestral: "Scènes poétiques" (1879); "Diane," *dr. poem* (1880); Symphonie ballet (1882); Gothic symphony; Overture dramatique (1883); "Symphonie Orientale" (1884); "Symphonie legendaire" (1886); orchestral suites "Lanterne Magique," "Brésilienne;" "Sur la Montagne;" "Kermesse;" "Tasse," *dr. sym.* in three parts for solo voices, chor. and orch. (prize of City of Paris, with Dubois' "Le Paradise Perdu," 1878).

Concertos: two violin concertos—No. 2, "Concerto Romantique" (1876); piano concerto (1878).

Chamber music: Sonata for 'cello and piano; Scènes Ecossaies for oboe and piano; sonatas for violin and piano; piano trio; string quartet.

Many piano pieces; "L'Aurore," for bass and orchestra (1882); over one hundred songs.

See H. Imbert's study in "Médaillons contemporains" (Paris, 1903).

GOUNOD, CHARLES FRANÇOIS

Born at Paris, June 17, 1818; died at Saint-Cloud, October 17, 1893. Pupil of Reicha; then of Halévy and Lesueur at the Paris Conservatory; prix de Rome, 1839. Organist and conductor of the Missions. Conductor of the Orphéon. Member of the Institute, 1866.

Operas: "Sapho," *op.* 3 *a.* (*Opé.*, 1851); "La Nonne Sanglante," *op.* 5 *a.* (*Opé.*, 1854); "La Colombe" (Baden, 1860); "Le Médecin Malgré lui," 3 *a.* (Th. Lyrique, 1858); "Faust," 5 *a.* (Th. Lyrique, 1859); "Philémon et Baucis," 3 *a.* (Th. Lyrique, 1860); "La Reine de Saba," 5 *a.* (*Opé.*, 1862); "Mireille" (Th. Lyrique, 1864); "Roméo et Juliette," 5 *a.* (Th. Lyrique); "Cinq-Mars," 4 *a.* (Op. C., 1877); "Polyeucte," *op.* 5 *a.* (*Opé.*, 1878); "Le Tribut de Zamora," 4 *a.* (*Opé.*, 1881). Stage music to "Ulysse," (1852); "Les Deux Reines" (1872); "Jeanne d'Arc" (1873). Oratorios: "Tobie" (Lyons, 1854); "Gallia" (London, 1871); "The Redemption" (Birmingham, 1882); "Mors et Vita" (Birmingham, 1885). Masses, cantatas, motets, psalms, choruses, symphonies, orchestral pieces, chamber music, songs, piano pieces. Author of method for Cor à pistons; "Etude sur le 'Don Juan' de Mozart;" "Etude sur 'Ascanio' de St. Saëns" (1889); "Mémoires d'un artiste" (1897). See "Notice," by H. Delaborde (1894); also by Th. Dubois (1894); "Ch. Gounod et son œuvre," by L. Pagnerre (1890).

HAHN, REYNALDO

Born at Caracas, Venezuela, August 9, 1874. Pupil of Massenet at the Paris Conservatory, he took minor prizes 1888–91. "I'le du rêve," 3 *a.* (Paris, 1898); "La Carmélite," *mus. com.* 4 *a.* (1902); "Nuit bergamesque," *sym. p.* (1897); incidental music to Daudet's "L'Obstacle" (1890).

HOLMÈS, AUGUSTA MARY ANNE

Born at Paris of Irish parentage, December 16, 1847; naturalized Frenchwoman in March, 1879; died at Paris, January 28, 1903. Pupil of Lambert (Versailles), Klosé and César Franck.

Operas: "Héro et Leandre" (Opéra Populaire, 1874); "Les Argonautes" (concert performance, 1881); "La Montagne Noire," *lyr. dr.* 4 *a.* (*Opé.*, 1895).

Psalm "In Exitu" (1873); "Astarte," *ov.* (1875); Andante Pastorale from a sym. "Orlando Furioso" (1877); "Lutèce," sym. (2d prize, City of Paris), 1st performance at Angers (1884); "Pologne," *sym. p.*; "Irlande," *sym. p.* (1882); "Pro Patria Ludus," *sym. ode* for ch. and orch. (after a mural picture by Puvis de Chavannes — Conservatory concert, 1888); "Triomphe de la République," triumphal ode (Palais de l'Industrie, 1889); "Hymne à la Paix," for Dante and Beatrice Festival (Florence, 1890); "Au Pays bleu," orch. suite (1891); "Hymne à Apollo," solo voices, ch. and orch. (1899); "Andromède," *sym. p.* (1900); "Veni Creator;" "Les Sept Ivresses;" "Vision de Sainte Thérèse" (1889); "La Vision de la Reine," *cant.*; music to Bordese's cycle "Contes Mystiques;" a setting of poems by Catullus; a hundred or more songs, some of them signed by her "Hermann Zenta."

Henri Gauthier-Villars wrote of her in 1889: "Somebody spoke of her as 'a pretentious blue-stocking.' Oh, no! She wears boots, boots with spurs on them. She is certainly not a woman in her use of the brass in the 'Ode Triomphale;' here she is a whole regiment; and at any rate she may justly be called, 'La Fiancée du Cymbalier.'"

See Villiers de l'Isle-Adam in "Chez les Passants;" Imbert's "Nouveaux Profils de Musiciens" (Paris, 1892); Saint-Saëns "Harmonie et Mélodie" (pp. 225–239).

HÜE, GEORGES ADOLPHE

Born at Versailles, May 6, 1858. Pupil of Reber and Paladilhe at the Paris Conservatory; prix de Rome, 1879; Cressent prize, 1881; City of Paris prize, 1885. "Les Pantins," *op. c.* 2 *a.* (1881); "Rubezahl," *sym. leg.* (1886); "Résurrection," sacred episode (1892); "Le Berger," ballad; Fantasia for violin (1893); stage music for "La Belle au bois dormant" (1894); "Cœur brisé," *pant.* (1890); "Le Roi de Paris," *op.* 3 *a.* (1901); "Titania," 1903; Symphony (1882); "Resurrection," sacred episode (1890–92); "Sommeil d'Hercule" (1892); "Kunesse," *cant.* (1897); "Scenes de Ballet" for orch. (1897).

See an elaborate biographical sketch in the *Musical Courier* (N. Y.), May 15, 1901.

INDY, PAUL MARIE THÉODORE VINCENT D'

Born at Paris, March 27, 1852.[1] Studied for the bar against his will, and preferred the lessons in harmony of Lavignac and the piano lessons of Diémer. Served during the Franco-Prussian War, then became connected with Colonne's Concerts du Châtelet as kettledrummer, afterward chorus-master. Entered the Paris Conservatory to study the organ with César Franck: 1st accessit, 1875. He then left the Conservatory to study counterpoint and composition with Franck. In 1887 he became chorus-master of the Lamoureux concerts and he helped prepare the first performance of "Lohengrin" in Paris (Eden Théâtre, May 3, 1887). One of the founders of the Société Nationale de Musique, he became president after the death of Franck. He was one of the founders in 1896 of the Schola Cantorum, of which he is now director. He was a Wagnerite of the early seventies. As conductor, he has travelled extensively.

Stage works: "Attendez moi sous l'orme," 1 *a.* (*comp.* 1876–78; Op. C., 1882); "Fervaal," musical action in 3 *a.* and a prologue (*comp.* 1889–95; Monnaie, Brussels, 1897); "L'Etranger," musical action (Brussels, 1903);

---

[1] *Date given me by the composer. "1851" is the year in the records of the Paris Conservatory.*

incidental music to Alexandre's "Karadec" (1891); to Mendès' tragedy "Médée" (1898).

Orchestral works: "La Foret Enchantée," *sym. ballad* (1878); "Wallenstein," trilogy after Schiller (*comp.* 1873–81); "Piccolomini" (*perf.* 1874); "Mort de Wallenstein" (*perf.* 1880); "Le Camp" (1884; first performance as a whole, 1888); "Saugefleurie," legend (*comp.* 1884; *perf.* 1885); symphony for piano and orch. on a French mountain air (*comp.* in 1886; *perf.* in 1887); Fantaisie on folk-songs for oboe and orch. (1888); "Istar," symphonic variations (*comp.* 1896; *perf.* Brussels, 1897); varied choral for saxophone and orch. (1903); symphony in B flat, 1904). Suite from the music to "Médée."

Chamber works: piano quartet (1878); suite in D in the old style for trumpet, two flutes and strings (1886); trio for piano, clarinet, 'cello (1886–87); 1st string quartet (1890); 2d string quartet (1897–98); "Chanson et Danses," for wind instruments (1898).

Vocal works: "La Chevauchée du Cid," scene for bar. and orch. (composed as a song 1877; remodelled and performed in 1884); "Le Chant de la Cloche," *dr. leg* after Schiller — City of Paris prize of 1886 — (*comp.* 1879–83; *perf.* 1886); "Clair de Lune," voice and orch. (1880); "Ste. Marie Magdeleine," *cant.* (1885); "Sur la Mer," chorus for female voices (1888); "Deus Israel," motet (1896); "Lied maritime," for voice and orch. (1896); a few songs.

Piano pieces: "Poème des Montagnes," suite (1881); "Helvetia," three waltzes (1884); "Schumanniana," three pieces (1887); "Tableaux de voyage," thirteen pieces (1889).

"La Chanson des Aventuriers de la Mer," bar. and orch. (1870); "Symphonie chevaleresque: Jean Hunyade" (1876); overture "Antoine et Cléopâtre" (1877), are not included by M. d'Indy in the manuscript catalogue drawn up by him, nor is the cantata for the inauguration of Augier's statue at Valence (1893).

D'Indy is the librettist of his two serious operas, a collaborator with Tiersot in collections of folk-songs, the editor of Solomon Rossi's madrigals, and the author of a "Cours de Composition musicale," of which only the first volume has been published as yet — 1904.

See Imbert's "Profils de Musiciens" (Paris, 1888); "'Fervaal' devant la Presse" (Paris, 1897); "Fervaal," by Etienne Destranges (Paris, 1896).

LALO, EDOUARD VICTOR ANTOINE

Born at Lille, January 27, 1823; died at Paris, April 23, 1892. Studied at Lille with Baumann; at Paris with Habeneck (violin), Schulhoff and Crèvecœur (composition). Viola of the Armingaud-Jacquard Quartet.

Stage works: "Fiesque," *op.* 3 *a.* (1867, not *perf.*); "Namouna," ballet, 2 *a.* (*Opé.*, 1882); "Le Roi d'Ys," *op.* 3 *a.* (*Op. C.*, 1888); "Néron," *pant.* (1891); "La Jacquerie," *op.* 4 *a.* (only the first act — completed by Coquard; Monte Carlo, 1895).

Orchestral: "Divertissement" (1872); Allegro; "Rapsodie Norvégienne" (1879); Symphony in G minor (1887).

Concertos: violin, op. 20 (1874); "Symphonie Espagnole," with violin solo, op. 21 (1875); 'cello (1877); "Fantaisie Norvégienne," for violin (Berlin, 1878); "Concerto Russe," for violin (1880); piano, in C minor (1889); "Fantaisie Ballet," for violin (first played in 1900).

Chamber and piano music. Among these pieces three piano trios, violin sonata, 'cello sonata, string quartet.

Three vocal pieces for church; about thirty songs; two duets.

See essays by Georges Servières; "La Musique française Moderne" (1897), and by H. Imbert in "Nouveaux Profils de Musiciens" (Paris, 1892).

LEMAIRE, JEAN EUGÈNE GASTON

Born at the Château d'Amblainvilliers (S. and O.), September 9, 1854. Pupil of the Ecole Niedermeyer. Music critic of *la Presse* (1888). "En dansant la gavotte: scène Louis XV chantée et dansée" (1890); operettas, ballets and pantomimes for minor theatres, "Jessick," *sym. p.*; pieces for orchestra, piano pieces, songs, sacred music.

LEROUX, XAVIER HENRI NAPOLEON

Born at Velletri, Papal States, October 11, 1863. Pupil of Dubois and Massenet at Paris Conservatory; 1st harmony prize (1881); 1st counterpoint and fugue prize (1884); prix de Rome, 1885. Teacher of harmony at the Conservatory. "Evangeline," *lyr. dr.* 4 *a.* (Brussels, 1895); "Astarté," *op.* 4 *a.* (1901); "La Reine Fiamette," dramatic tale, 5 *a.* (1903); "Endymion," *cant.*; incidental music to Sardou and Moreau's "Cléopâtre" (1890); Æschylus' "Persians" (1896); mass with orchestra; "Harold," *dr. or.* (1892); "Venus et Adonis;" "William Ratcliff;" motets, songs.

MASSENET, JULES EMILE FRÉDÉRIC

Born May 12, 1842, at Montaud (Loire). Pupil of Laurent (piano), Reber (composition), at the Paris Conservatory; 1st prize for piano, 1859; counterpoint and fugue, 1863; prix de Rome, 1863. Professor of composition at the Conservatory, 1878–96. Member of the Institute, 1878.

Operas: "La Grand'tante," *op. c.* 1 *a.* (1867); "Don César de Bazan," *op. c.* 3 *a.* (1872); "L'Adorable Bel-Boul," operet. 1 *a.* (1874); "Bérengère et Anatole," operet. 1 *a.* (1876); "Le Roi de Lahore," *op.* 5 *a.* (1877); "Hérodiade," *op.* 5 *a.* (Brussels, 1881); "Manon," *op.* 5 *a.* (1884); "Werther," *op.* 3 *a.* (*comp.* in 1884; produced at Vienna, 1892); "Le Cid," *op.* 5 *a.* (1885); "Esclarmonde," legendary *lyr. dr.* 4 *a.* (1889); "Le Mage," *op.* 5 *a.* (1891); "Le Carillon," ballet (Vienna, 1892); "Thais," *op.* 3 *a.* (1894); "Le Portrait de Manon," *op. c.* 1 *a.* (1894); "La Navarraise," *lyr. dr.* 2 *a.* (London, 1895); "Sapho," lyric piece, 5 *a.* (1897); "Cendrillon," fairy tale, 4 *a.* (1899); "Griselidis," lyric tale, 3 a. (1901); "Le Jongleur de Notre-Dame," miracle, 3 a. (Monte Carlo, 1902).

Stage music: to Leconte de Lisle's "Les Erinnyes" (1873); Déroulède's "Hetman" (1877); Porto-Riche's "Drame sous Philippe II" (1877); to Sardou's "Théodora" (1884) and "Le Crocodile" (1886); Racine's "Phèdre" (1900); "Le Grillon du Foyer" (1904).

Cantatas, etc.: "Paix et Liberté" (1867); "Marie Magdeleine," sacred drama (1873); "Eve," mystery (1875); "Narcisse," antique idyl (1878); "La Vierge," sacred legend (1880); "Biblis," antique scene (1887); "La Terre promise," or. (1900); two choruses for male voices: "Le Moulin" and "Alleluia" (1866); several other choruses, a Requiem Mass (unpublished), and a few small pieces for church service.

Orchestral: concert overture (1863); overture to "Phèdre" (1874); 1st suite (1867–68); 2d suite, "Scènes Hongroises" (1871); 3d suite, "Scènes Pittoresques" (1873); 4th suite, "Scènes Dramatiques," after Shakespeare (1875); 5th suite, "Scènes Napolitaines" (*comp.* in 1863; *perf.* 1880); 6th suite, "Scènes de Féerie" (London, 1881); 7th suite, "Scènes Alsaciennes" (1882); "Sarabande" (1877); "Marche de Szabady" (1879); "Visions," *sym. p.*; piano concerto; overture to "Brumaire" (1901).

Chamber music: "Dichetto," for strings and wind instruments (1872), 'cello pieces, and a few piano pieces; string quartet unpublished.

Songs: "Poème d'Avril" (1866); "Poème du Souvenir," "Poème Pastoral," "Poème d'Octobre," "Poème d'Amour," "Poème d'hiver;" over one hundred songs and a few duets.

See "Massenet," by E. de Solenière (1897); G. Servières' "La Musique française moderne" (1897); H. Imbert's "Profils d'artistes contemp." (1897).

PALADILHE, ÉMILE

Born at Montpellier, June 3, 1844. Pupil of Marmontel, Benoist and Halévy at the Paris Conservatory: 1st piano prize, 1857; prix de Rome, 1860. "Le Chevalier Bernard" (1858); "La Reine Mathilde" (1859); "Le Passant," *op. c.* 1 *a.* (1872); "L'Amour Africain," *op. c.* 2 *a.* (1875); "Suzanne," *op. c.* 3 *a.* (1878); "Diana," *op. c.* 3 *a.* (1885); "Patrie," *op.* 5 *a.* (1886); "Les Saintes Maries de la Mer," *lyr. dr.* (Montpellier, 1892). Symphony in E flat, overture, Messe Solennelle, Messe de Saint-François d'Assise (1896), piano pieces, songs—the most famous of which is "Mandolinata."

PESSARD, ÉMILE LOUIS FORTUNÉ

Born at Montmartre (Seine), May 29, 1843. Pupil of Laurent, Benoist and Carafa at the Paris Conservatory: 1st harmony prize, 1862; prix de Rome, 1866. Teacher of harmony at the Conservatory. "La Cruche Cassée," *op. c.* 1 *a.* (1870); "Le Char," *op. c.* 1 *a.* (1878); "Le Capitaine Fracasse," *op. c.* 3 *a.* (1878); "Tabarin," *op. c.* 2 *a.* (1885); "Don Quichotte," *op. c.* 1 *a.* (1889); "Les Folies amoureuses," *op. c.* 3 *a.* (1891); "Mam'zelle Carabin," *op.* 3 *a.* (1893); "Le Muet" (1894); "La Dame de Trèfle" (1898). Stage music for "Tartarin sur les Alpes" (1888) and "Une Nuit de Noël" (1893); "Dalila," *cant.* (1867); masses, motets, orchestral suites, piano trio and other chamber music, songs.

PIERNÉ, HENRI CONSTANT GABRIEL

Born at Metz, August 16, 1863. Pupil of Marmontel, Franck, Massenet at the Paris Conservatory: 1st prizes: piano, 1879; organ, 1882; counterpoint and fugue, 1881; prix de Rome (second grand prix), 1882. Organist of Ste. Clotilde (1890–98).

Stage works: "Le Collier de Saphirs," *pant.* 2 *a.* (Spa, 1891); "Les joyeuses commères de Paris," *fant.* 5 *a.* (1892); "Pierre poète," *pant.* 2 *a.* (1892); "Bouton d'or," *fant.* 4 *a.* (1893); "Le Docteur Blanc," *mim.* 5 *a.* (1893); music to Lorrain's "Yanthis" (1894); to Silvestre and Morand's "Izëil" (1894); to Rostand's "La Princesse lointaine" (1895); to "Salomé," *lyr. pant.*, by Silvestre and Meltzer for Loie Fuller (1895); "La Coupe enchantée," *op. c.* 2 *a.* (Royan, 1895); "Vendée," *lyr. dr.* 3 *a.* (Lyons, 1897); "La Fille de Tabarin," *lyr. com.* 3 *a.* (1901).

"Nuit de Noël, 1870," *lyr. ep.* (1895); "L'an mil," *sym. p.* with chorus (1898); "Deux Contes de Jean Lorrain," orch. (1896); Hymn to the Russian Visitors (1893); "The Gallic Muse," solo voices, ch. piano; piano concerto in C minor; sonata for violin and piano.

ROPARTZ, J. GUY

Born June 15, 1864, at Guingamp. Studied for the bar at Rennes. Pupil of Dubois and Massenet at the Paris Conservatory, which he left to study with César Franck. Poet, critic, essayist, dramatist. Appointed director of the Conservatory of Nancy in 1894; conductor of the Conservatory of Nancy concerts. Incidental music for Loti and Tiercelin's "Pêcheur d'Islande" (1893); Tiercelin's "Le Diable Couturier" (1894), "Kéruzel" (1895) and for "Famille et Petrie" (1891).

Orchestral: Symp. No. 1 on a Breton Choral (1895), Symp. No. 2. Two suites from "Pêcheur d'Islande," "Les Landes," "Passage Breton," Fantaisie in D major (1898); Cinq pièces brèves, "Dimanche Breton," suite; "Le Convoi du Fermier," "Carnaval," "Marche de Fête."

"Psalm cxxxvi," for ch. organ and orch. (Nancy, 1898); church pieces, string quartet in G minor (1894); "Prière," for bar. and orch.; adagio for 'cello and orch. (1899); "Lamento," for oboe and orch.; "Quatre Poèmes" (after Heine's "Intermezzo"), for bar. and orch. (Nancy, 1899); "Les Fileuses de Bretagne," for fem. ch.; piano pieces, among them a piece in B minor for two pianos (Nancy, 1899); organ pieces, songs.

ROTHSCHILD, BARONESS WILLY DE

Amateur, and composer of fashionable nocturnes and melodies.

BIOGRAPHICAL SKETCHES

SAINT-SAËNS, CHARLES CAMILLE
Born at Paris, October 9, 1835. Studied with Stamaty (piano), Maleden (composition), and then was a pupil of Benoist and Halévy at the Conservatory: 1st prize for organ, 1851. Organist of Saint-Méry (1853-58); of La Madeleine (1858-77); professor at the Ecole Niedermeyer; wandering piano virtuoso; member of the Institute, 1881.

Operas: "La Princesse Jaune," 1 a. (*Op. C.*, 1872); "Le Timbre d'argent," 4 a. (Th. Lyrique, 1877); "Samson et Dalila," *op*. 3 a. (Weimar, 1877); "Etienne Marcel," 4 a. (Lyons, 1879); "Henri VIII," 5 a. (*Opé.*, 1883); "Proserpine," 4 a. (*Op. C.*, 1887); "Ascanio," 5 a. (*Opé.*, 1890); "Phryné," 2 a. (*Op. C.*, 1893); "Frédégonde," completion of Guiraud's opera, 5 a. (*Opé.*, 1895); "Lola," *dr. sc.*, orchestrated by Ch. Koechlin (1901); "Les Barbares," *lyr. tr.*, prologue and 3 a. (1901); "Hélène" (Monte Carlo, 1904).

Other stage music: Restoration of Charpentier's music to Molière's "Le Malade imaginaire" (1892); chorus and intermezzi to Sophocles' "Antigone"—Vacquerie and Meurice—(1893); "Javotte," ballet (Lyons, 1896); to Gallet's "Déjanire" (Béziers, 1898); to Jane Dieulafoy's "Parysatis" (Béziers, 1902).

Oratorios, etc.: "Oratorio de Noël" (1858); Scene d'"Horace"—Corneille's tragedy—(1866); "Les Noces de Prométhée," *cant*. (1867); "Cœli enarrant," Psalm xix (1873); "Le Deluge," biblical poem (1876); "La Lyre et la Harpe" (Birmingham, 1879); "La Fiancée du Timbalier," ballad (1887); "Pallas Athénè" (Orange, 1894); "La Feu Celeste," *cant*. (1900).

Religious music: Mass (1857); "Tantum ergo;" Requiem Mass (1878); twenty motets, etc.

Orchestral: 1st sym. (1853), 2d (*comp*. 1862; *perf*. 1880), 3d (London, 1886); "Le Rouet d'Omphale," *sym. p*. (1872); "Phaéton," *sym. p*. (1873); "Danse Macabre," *sym. p*. (1875); "La Jeunesse d'Hercule" (1877); Suite (1863-77); "Suite Algérienne" (1879-80); "Marche Héroique" (1870); "Hymne à Victor Hugo" (1884); "Rapsodie d'Auvergne," piano and orch. (1885); "Africa," piano and orch. (1891); Tarantelle for flute and clarinet with orch. (1857); Introduction and Rondo Capriccioso for violin and orch. (1867).

Concertos: Piano: No. 1, D major (1862); No. 2, G minor (1868); No. 3, E♭ (1870); No. 4, C minor (1875); No. 5 (1896). Violin: No. 1, A major (1859-68); No. 2, C major (1858-60); No. 3, B minor (1880-81). 'Cello: No. 1 (1873); No. 2 (1903).

Chamber music: piano quintet, A minor (1855-65); piano quartet (1875); 1st piano trio, F major, (1863-67); 2d piano trio (1892); 1st violin sonata, D minor (1885); 2d violin sonata in E♭ major (1896); 'cello sonata in C minor (1872); trumpet septet (1881); string quartet in E minor (1899).

Songs, organ pieces, piano pieces, etc.

Author of "Harmonie et Mélodie," essays (1885); "Note sur les décors de théâtre dans l'antiquité romaine" (1886); "Problèmes et Mystères," philosophical reflections (1894); "Portraits et souvenirs" (Paris, *s.d.*); "Rimes familières;" comedies which have been played, as "La Crampe des écrivains" (Algiers, 1892), and published. Music critic, essayist and pamphleteer.

See O. Neitzel's "Camille Saint-Saëns" (Berlin, 1899); Imbert's "Profils de Musiciens" (Paris, 1888); Servières' "La Musique Française moderne" (Paris, 1897).

THOMAS, CHARLES LOUIS AMBROISE
Born at Metz, August 5, 1811; died at the Paris Conservatory, February 12, 1896. Pupil of Lesueur, Zimmerman, Dourlan at the Paris Conservatory: 1st prize, piano, 1829; harmony, 1830; prix de Rome, 1832. Professor of composition and then Director of the Conservatory. Member of the Institute, 1837. Twenty-three operas of which the chief are "Le Caïd" (*Op. C.*, 1849); "Le Songe d'une nuit d'été" (*Op. C.*, 1850); "Raymond" (*Op. C.*, 1851); "Mignon," 3 a. (*Op. C.*, 1866); "Hamlet," 5 a. (*Opé.*, 1868); "Francoise de Rimini," 5 a. (*Opé.*, 1882); "La Tempête" (*Opé.*, 1889). Cantata for dedication of Lesueur's statue (1852); "Hommage à Boïeldieu" (1875); piano trios, quartets, quintets, masses, motets, choruses, songs, pieces for organ, etc. See "Notice," by Delaborde (1896).

THOMÉ, FRANÇOIS LUC JOSEPH (called FRANCIS)
Born at Port Louis (Mauritius), October 18, 1850. Pupil of Marmontel and Duprato at the Paris Conservatory: 2d prize for piano, 1869; 2d prize for harmony, 1869; 1st prize for counterpoint and fugue, 1870. Composer of ballets, pantomimes, operettas; "Mlle. Pygmalion," *pant*. 3 a. (1895); of much stage music, from that of "Romeo et Juliette" (1890) to that of "Quo Vadis" (1901); ode symphonique "Hymne à la nuit;" piano pieces, songs. Teacher and music critic.

WIDOR, CHARLES MARIE
Born at Lyons, February 22, 1845. Studied at Lyons, then at Brussels with Lemmens and Fétis. Organist at Lyons; organist of Saint-Sulpice, Paris, since 1869. Succeeded César Franck as professor of the organ at the Paris Conservatory, and in 1896 became professor of composition, counterpoint and fugue at that institution. Music critic of *L'Estafette*. Stage works: "La Korrigane," ballet (*Opé.*, 1880); "Conte d'Avril" (after Shakespeare), incidental music (1885); incidental music to Coppée's "Les Jacobites" (1885); "Maître Ambros," *lyr. dr*. 4 a. (1896); "Jeanne d'Arc," *pant*. 3 a. (1890). Orchestral and chamber music, organ pieces with and without orchestra, piano music and songs.

See Imbert's "Portraits et Études" (Paris, 1894).

MODERN FRENCH SONGS
VOLUME II

GAVOTTE OF THE MASQUERADE
(GAVOTTE DU MASQUE)

(Original Key)

MONTJOYEUX
Translated by Isabella G. Parker

ALEXANDRE GEORGES
(1850 —

A mask thy face con-ceal—ing, Prin-cess with tim-id air, To seek what lov-er fair, Thus per-fumed, art thou

Où cou-rez-vous mas-qué—e Prin-cesse à l'air peu-reux, Et pour quel a-mou-reux Vous ê-tes-vous mus-

Copyright MCMIV by Oliver Ditson Company

ML-537-4

COME AND EMBARK!
(EMBARQUEZ-VOUS!)

ULRICH GUTTINGUER
Translated by Charles Fonteyn Manney

(Original Key)

BENJAMIN GODARD
(1849–1895)

Copyright MCMIV by Oliver Ditson Company

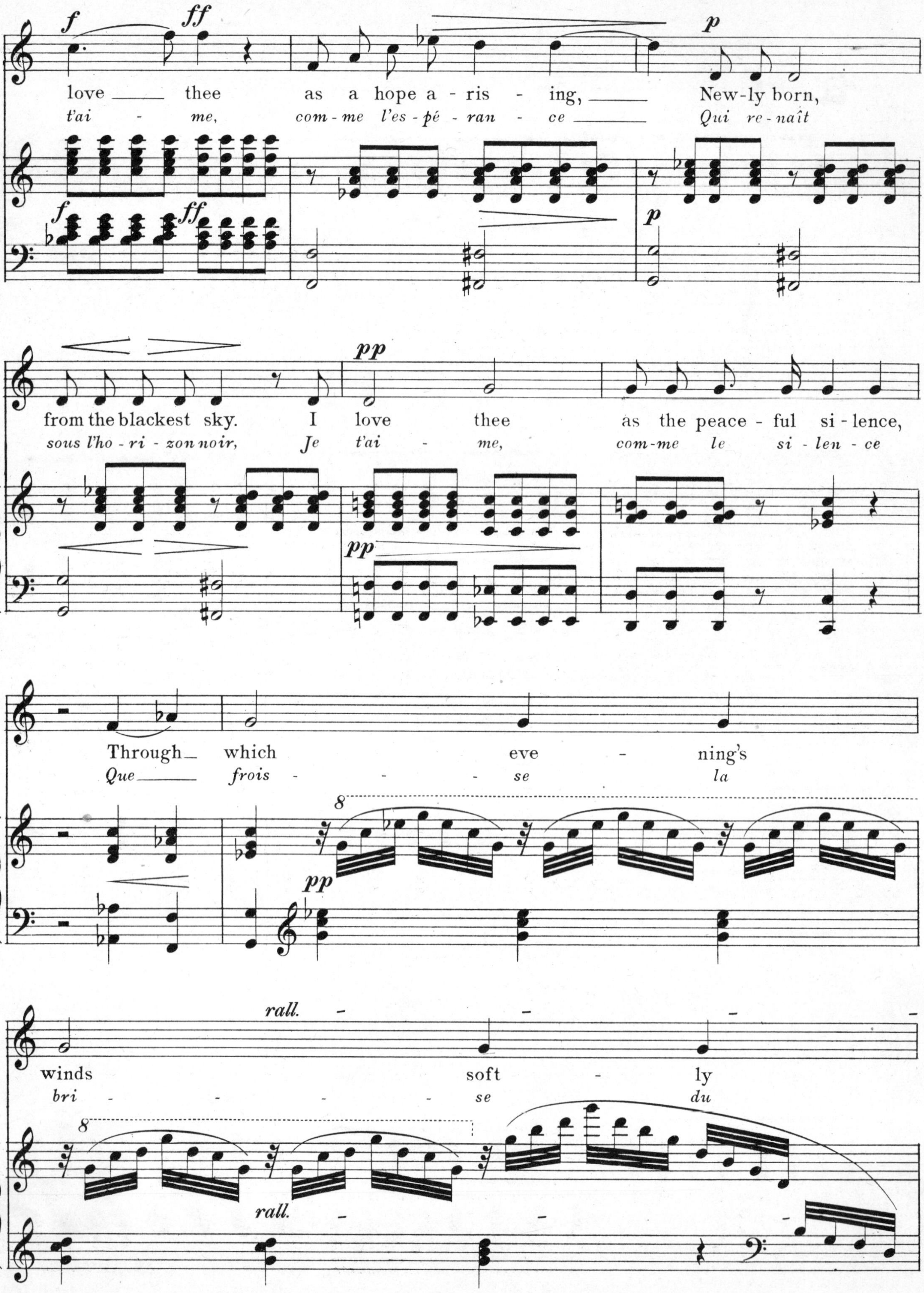
f
ff
p
love thee as a hope a-ris-ing, New-ly born,
t'ai-me, com-me l'es-pé-ran-ce Qui re-naît
from the blackest sky. I love thee as the peace-ful si-lence,
sous l'ho-ri-zon noir, Je t'ai-me, com-me le si-len-ce
pp
Through which eve-ning's
Que frois-se la
rall.
winds soft-ly
bri-se du

a tempo
p
sigh. I love thee
soir; Je t'ai - me,
sf a tempo
f
p
as some wild-rose blos - som, Low in - clin - ing with state-ly
com - me l'é-glan - ti - ne Qui se penche a - vec ma - jes -
f
cresc.
f
dim.
air; As the fra-grance sweet of the haw-thorn, Or these young elms I plant with
té; Com-me la su - ave au - bé - pi - ne, Com - me l'or - meau que j'ai plan -
cresc.
f
dim.
p
pp
cresc.
f
care. I love thee, I love thee, I
té; Je t'ai - me, je t'ai - me, je
p
pp
cresc.

16

love ___ thee, e'en as my soul de-vot - ed   Lov-ing-ly longs
t'ai   me en-fin com-me mon â - me   Ai-me d'am-our

for heav'n a-bove;   As doth an an-gel fair and ho - ly   Ev-er-
le beau ciel bleu,   Com-me le ché-ru-bin en flam - me   À ja-

more his Cre - a - tor love.
mais ai - me - ra   son Dieu!

To Mme. Conneau
TO SPRING
(AU PRINTEMPS)

(Composed in Rome, about 1840)

JULES BARBIER (1825-)
Translated by Charles Fonteyn Manney

CHARLES GOUNOD
(1818-1893)

Animato *(Animé et avec entraînement)*

Win-ter yields to the wiles of spring,
Le prin-temps chas-se les hi-vers

In the for-est the bird-lings sing,
Et sou-rit dans les ar-bres verts

Ver-dant mead-ows are gay a-new with
Sous la feuil-le nou-vel-le pas-sent

Copyright MCMIV by Oliver Ditson Company

bud and blos - som.
des bruits d'ai - le!

Let us roam in the sha - dy grove,
Viens, sui - vons les sen - tiers om - breux,

Breath - ing vows of deep - est love.
Où s'é - ga - rent les a - mou - reux,

Spring in - vites us with smiles To joys be -
Le prin - temps nous ap - pel - le Viens, so -

yond com - pare.
yons heu - reux.

incalzando
(chaud et contenu)

Bright - ly the sun - beams are glanc - ing,
Vois! le so - leil é - tin - cel - le,

In thy dear eyes bright - er danc - ing,
Et sa clar - té qui ruis - sel - le,

Mak - ing still more en - tranc - ing Thy
Me sem - ble en - cor plus bel - le Dans

beau - ty rare.
tes beaux yeux!

Let us roam in the sha - dy grove,
Viens, sui - vons les sen - tiers om - breux,

Breath - ing vows of deep - est love.
Où s'é - ga - rent les a - mou - reux,

Spring in - vites us with smiles To joys be -
Le prin - temps nous ap - pel - le, Viens, so -

21

yond com-pare. Let thy sweet voice, up-ward
yons heu-reux! Que ta voix chante et se

soar-ing, Join with the lark's out-pour-ing,
mê-le A l'har-mo-nie é-ter-nel-le.

Rais-ing a song a-dor-ing Thro' skies so
Je crois en-ten-dre en el-le chan-ter les

fair. Let us roam in the shad-y grove,
cieux! Viens sui-vons les sen-tiers om-breux,

M L - 541 - 6

Breath-ing vows__ of deep-est love. Spring in-vites us with smiles To joys__ be-yond com-pare.__

Où s'é-ga-rent les a-mou-reux. Le prin-temps nous ap-pel-le. Viens, so-yons heu-reux!__

À Madame Jules Barbier

MEDJÉ
(AN ARABIAN SONG)
(CHANSON ARABE)

JULES BARBIER (1825 -)
Translated by Arthur Westbrook

CHARLES GOUNOD
(1818 - 1893)

O Medjé,[*] en-chain'd I'm yield-ing, To thy smile a will-ing slave; As em-press thy scep-tre wield-ing, My free-dom to thee I gave. No more my glad way pur-su-ing, Like

Ô Med-jé, qui d'un sou-ri-re En-chai-nas ma li-ber-té. Sois fiè-re de ton em-pi-re Com-mande à ma vo-lon-té. Na-guère en-cor, sans en-tra-ves, Com-

[*] Pronounce, "Měd-yea"

Copyright MCMIV by Oliver Ditson Company

some wild bird of the sea,— I must heed thy glance sub-du-ing, Who
me l'oi-seau dans les airs,— Ton re-gard a fait es-cla-ve Le

roam'd the wide des-ert free.— Med - jé!— Med - jé!— The
libre en-fant des dé-serts.— Med - jé!— Med - jé!— La

voice— of love's e-mo-tion Should thy— com-pas-sion move!— A-
voix— de l'a-mour mê-me De-vrait te dés-ar-mer!— Hé-

las!— Why doubt my heart's de-vo-tion, When I die for thy
las!— Tu dou-tes que je l'ai-me Quand je meurs de t'ai-

love! ___ When I die for thy love! ___
mer! ___ Quands je meurs de t'ai - mer! ___

These rich gems, ___ thy charms en-hanc - ing, All with en-vy may be-
Ces bi - joux ___ que l'on t'en-vi - e J'ai ven-du pour les pa-

hold; ___ To pay for their bril-liant glanc - ing My
yer, ___ In - gra - te plus que ma vi - e, Mes

arms and my steed I sold!___ The spell is ev - er___
ar - mes et mon cour - sier!___ Et tu de-man - des quels

grow - ing, Which to thy side binds me fast.___ Dost not
char - mes Tien - nent mon coeur en - i - vré?___ Tu n'as

see my tears still flow - ing? Wilt thou not yield thee at
donc pas vu mes lar - mes? Tou - te la nuit j'ai pleu -

last?___ Med - jé!___ Med - jé!___ The
ré!___ Med - jé!___ Med - jé!___ Les

tears of love's e - mo - tion Should thy com-pas-sion
pleurs de l'a-mour mê - me De - vraient te dés-ar -
move! A - las!
mer! Hé - las!
estinto
Dost doubt my heart's de -
tu dou - tes que je
cre - scen - do
f
vo - tion, When I die for thy love!
t'ai - me Quand je meurs de t'ai - mer!
dim.
p
When I die for thy love!
Quand je meurs de t'ai - mer!
a tempo
pp
colla voce
cre -

28

If my heart___ thou wouldst be read - ing, Plunge this dag-ger in my breast!___ And while for thee it is bleed - ing, Thy name thou'lt find there im - press'd.___ Be - hold, then, in bright - ness

Tu veux li - re dans mon â - me pour y voir ton nom vain - queur!___ Eh bien! prends donc cet - te la - me Et plon - ge la dans mon coeur!___ Re - gar - de sans é - pou -

ML-542-8

shining, Thy soul un-moved as of yore,___ Thine own
van - te Et sans re-grets su-per-flus___ Ton i-

im-age fair, en-twin-ing With the heart___ that beats no
mago on-cor vi-van-te Dans ce coeur___ qui ne bat

more!___ Med-jé!___ Med-jé!___ My
plus!___ Med-jé!___ Med-jé!___ Le

blood,___ my last e-mo-tion Should thy___ com-pas-sion
sang___ de l'a-mour mê-me De-vrait___ te dés-ar-

move! ____ A - las! _____ Why doubt my heart's de-
mer! Hé - las! _____ Tu dou - tes que je

vo - tion, When I die for thy love! ____
t'ai - me, Quand je meurs de t'ai - mer! ____

When I die for thy love! ____
Quand je meurs de t'ai - mer! ____

THE VALLEY
(LE VALLON)

(Composed in Rome, about 1840)

ALPHONSE de LAMARTINE (1790-1869)
Translated by Arthur Westbrook

CHARLES GOUNOD
(1818-1893)

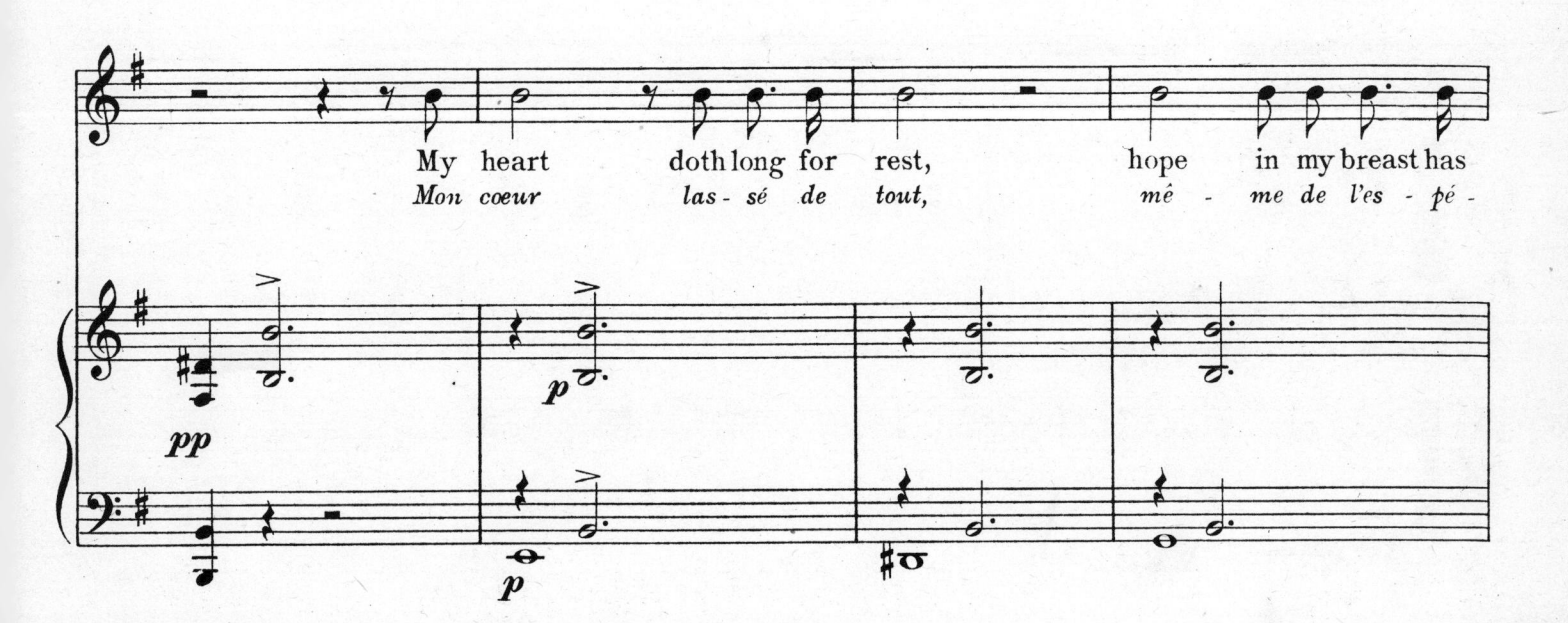

Andante quasi adagio

My heart doth long for rest, hope in my breast has faded; And no more do I crave joys which the fates deny! In the
Mon cœur lassé de tout, mê - me de l'es - pé - ran - ce, N'i - ra plus de ses vœux im - por - tu - ner le sort! Prê - tez-

Copyright MCMIV by Oliver Ditson Company

ML-543-7

home of my youth, the vale so green and shaded, Let an
-moi seu-le-ment, val-lon de mon en-fan-ce, Un a-

hour of re-pose bring me peace ere I
-si-le d'un jour pour at-ten-dre la

die.
mort!

My life seems like a
D'i-ci je vois la

33

34

a tempo

Rest thou, my soul, be pa-tient; here lies thy goal be-
Re - po - se - toi, mon â - me, en ce der - nier a -

fore thee, And like a Pil-grim worn, yet with
si - le Ain - si qu'un voy - a - geur qui, le

heart free from care, Pause at the o-pen gate, while
cœur plein d'es - poir S'as - sied a - vant d'en - trer, aux

Peace comes o-ver thee, And breathe for a while the balm-y eve-ning air,
por - tes de la ville Et res - pire un mo-ment l'air em - bau - mé du soir,

35

Yes, here breathe for a-while the balm-y eve-ning air!
Et res - pire un mo - ment l'air em - bau - mé du soir!

Thy
Tes

days draw to a close sad au-tumn winds are
jours tris - tes et courts com - me des jours d'au -

sigh-ing, While shades of com-ing night wrap the world in
tom - ne Dé - cli - nent com - me l'ombre au pen - chant des cô -

gloom.___ Friend-ship's vows are but false, And com-pas-sion is
teaux.___ L'a - mi - tié te tra-hit, la pi - tié t'a-ban-

ly-ing For-lorn___ And a-lone, seek the path to the
don - ne Et seu - le tu des-cends le sen - tier des tom-

tomb!___ No! still is Na-ture kind,___ let her love to thee ap-
beaux!___ Mais la na-ture est là___ qui t'in-vite_ et qui

peal,___ Be at rest, be at rest in her arms on her
t'ai - me Plon - ge-toi, plon - ge-toi dans son sein qu'el - le

37

THE PERFECT HOUR
(L'HEURE EXQUISE)
CHANSONS GRISES, N° 5

(Composed in 1892)

(Original Key, B)

PAUL VERLAINE (1844-1896)
Translated by Alexander Blaess

REYNALDO HAHN (1875-   )

Molto dolce e tranquillo
(Infiniment doux et calme)

The sil-v'ry moon-light Streams on the wood; O'er shim-m'ring cov-erts, From ev-'ry bough A voice is soar-ing, O well be-
La lu-ne blan-che Luit dans les bois; De cha-que bran-che Part u-ne voix Sous la ra-mé-e, O bien-ai-

delicatamente
(delicatement)

Copyright MCMIV by Oliver Ditson Company

ML-544-3

discrete
(discret)
p
lov - - - - - - - ed! A faith - ful
mé - - - - - - - e. L'é - tang re -
pp
mir - ror, The pond re - flects, A som - bre wil - -
flè - te, Pro - fond mi - roir, La sil - hou - et - -
low's black sil - hou - ette, Where weeps the wind. Fair dream!
te Du sau - le noir Où le vent pleu - re Rê - vons
pp
p
dim.
pp
oh lin - - - - ger!
c'est l'heu - - - - re.
ancor più p
(plus p encore)
p
pp

ancor più tranquillo
(*plus calme encore*)

A ten-der calm, in-fi-nite peace Droops from the moon-beams That o-pal-esce The vault of heav-en. Dwell, per-fect hour!

Un vaste et tendre A-pai-se-ment, Sem-ble des-cen-dre Du fir-ma-ment Que l'astre i-ri-se. C'est l'heure ex-qui-se.

rall.
(*rallentissez*)

col voce
(*suivez*)

a tempo

pp

senza rall.
(*sans retenir*)

pp

ppp

COULD MY SONGS THEIR WAY BE WINGING
(SI MES VERS AVAIENT DES AILES!)

VICTOR HUGO (1802-1885)
Translated by Charles Fonteyn Manney

REYNALDO HAHN
(1875-   )

Copyright MDCCCXCIX by Oliver Ditson Company

poco meno lento

Un-to thy hearth, up-ward spring-ing, They would fly with-out con-trol, Could my songs their way be wing-ing As doth the soul.

Il vo-le-raient, é-tin-cel-les Vers vo-tre foy-er qui rit, Si mes vers a-vaient des ai-les Com-me l'es-prit.

poco rit.
pp
a tempo

più lento, ritard. sin' al fine
pp
To thy heart a mes-sage sing - ing, All love and faith, dear, to
Près de vous, purs et fi - dè - - les, Ils ac-cour-raient, nuit et
pp
p
molto rit.
prove, Could my songs their way be wing - ing,
jour, Si mes vers a - vaient des ai - les,
colla voce
ancor più lento
pp
lunga
ppp
Lento
Could my songs their way be wing - ing As doth my love!
Si mes vers a-vaient des ai - les Com - me l'a - mour!
p
pp
ppp

A THRENODY
(THRÎNÓDIA)
CHANTS DE LA KITHARÈDE, Nº 3

(Original Key, E♭)

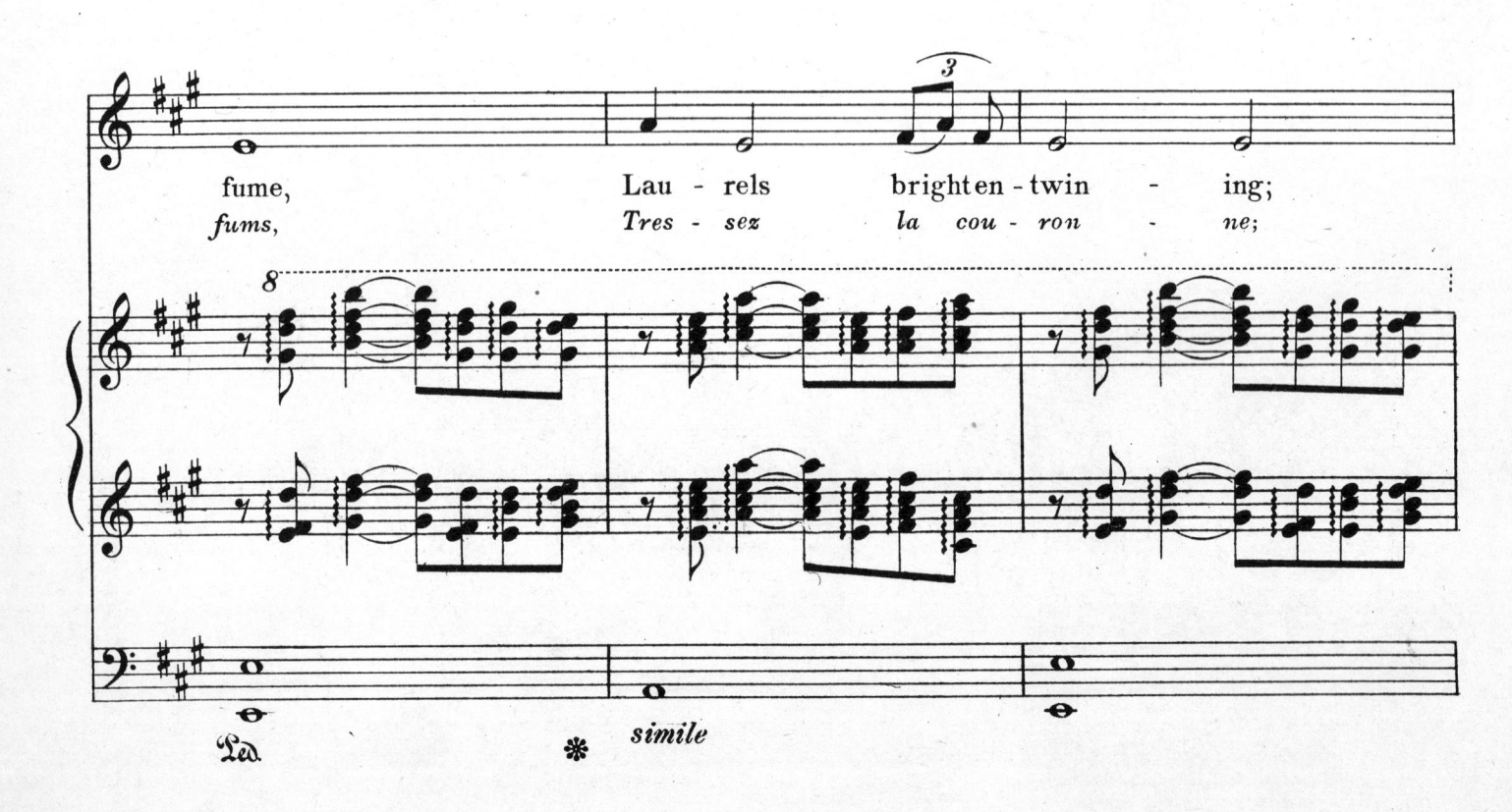

AUGUSTA HOLMÈS (1847–1903)
Translated by Isabella G. Parker

AUGUSTA HOLMÈS
(1847–1903)

For Se-le-né is shin-ing Thro' skies dark with gloom. Gold-en veil sur-round-ing My brows be hung; Let my lyre be

Sé-lé-né ray-on-ne Au fond des cieux bruns. Dé-co-rez ma tê-te D'un long voi-le d'or; Qu'à chan-ter en

strung, Sweet songs be re-sound - ing!
-cor Ma Ly - re soit prê - te!

Build my fu-n'ral pyre,
Tail - lez mon bû - cher

Out of oak pre-par - ing;
Dans le coeur des chê - nes;

cre - - scen - do
For chains I — am wear - ing Of the God of Fire! — A - pol - lo — at my por - tal His fair arms ex - tends! Weep not, O — my
Je por - te les chaî - nes Du di - vin Ar - cher! — Phoï - bos m'ap - pel - le Et me tend les — bras! Ne me pleu-rez
f
p
cre - scen - do
dim.
R.H.

friends! Weep not, O my friends!
pas, *Ne me pleu - rez pas,*

Since I am im - mor - - - tal! ____
Je suis im - mor - tel - - - le! ____

AN IRISH NOËL
(NOËL D'IRLANDE)

(Original Key, D)

AUGUSTA HOLMÈS (1847-1903)
Translated by Isabella G. Parker

AUGUSTA HOLMÈS
(1847-1903)

Oh, dream, — Oh, dream, — Chil-dren of E - rin, — Di - vine No - ël is bring-ing for you bread to eat! — Oh, dream, — Oh, dream, —

Rê - vez, — rê - vez, — En - fants d'Ir - lan - de, — Que le di - vin No - ël vous ap - por - te du pain! — Rê - vez, — rê - vez, —

Copyright MCMIV by Oliver Ditson Company

ML-547-4

in your own coun - try___ you shall warm at a fire_ of pine
que sur la lan - de___ Vous chauf - fez_ vos pieds nus aux flam -

your freez - ing feet!___ Oh, dream,___ Oh, dream,___
mes du sa - pin!__ Ré - vez,___ ré - vez,___

Sing - ers of E - rin,___ That the glo-rious time re - turn-eth a - gain of
Chan-teurs d'Ir - lan - de,___ Que les temps_ re - vien-dront des Hé - ros

he-roes and kings! Oh, dream, Oh, dream, that
et des Rois! Rê - vez, ré - vez que

God com-mand - eth, And now the Cross, the Tre-foil and Harp
Dieu com - man - de Et qu'il vous rend la Harpe, et le Trè-

to you He brings! Oh, dream, Oh, dream,
fle, et la Croix. Rê - vez, ré - vez,

Martyrs of E - rin, __ That the day __ comes of glo - ry and e - qui -
Mar-tyrs d'Ir lan - de, __ Que le jour __ est ve - nu de gloi - re et d'é - qui -

ty! __ Oh, dream, __ No - ël to you re - stor -
té! __ Ré - vez! __ Et que No - ël vous ren -

eth __ The pow'r of your fore - fa - thers and Lib - er - ty!
de __ La for - ce des aï - eux a - vec la Li - ber - té!

MEMORIES OF YORE
(BRISES D'AUTREFOIS)

(Composed about 1896)

HENRY GAUTHIER-VILLARS
Translated by Alexander Blaess

GEORGES HÜE
(1858-   )

On the wall, gems of an-cient fab-rics Re-tain the sun-set's sump-tuous glow; And thy low voice re-calls a song. Me-

Les é - tof - fes au mur ten - du - es S'al - lu - ment au so - leil cou - chant; Et ta voix douce est comme un chant Plein

Copyright MCMIV by Oliver Ditson Company

lo - dious stan - zas ne'er for - got - ten, Heard of yore, in the sun -
de pa - ro - les en - ten - du - es, Au - tre - fois, au so - leil

set's glow, In the park when we oft pa -
cou - chant, Dans les parcs ou nous pro - me -

rad - ed The haugh - ty pride of our new bliss, With firm be -
nâ - mes L'or - gueil d'un jeune en - chan - te - ment, Dans la croy -

lief in the sweet bond, That our young souls for e'er were plight - ing:
an - ce du ser - ment Dont nous a - vons li - é nos â - mes:

Oh, the su-preme, th'en-rap-tured bliss!
Ô le su-prême en-chan-te-ment!

There lin-gers in thy heav-y tress-es Sweet-est fra-grance, dear in the past;
Il pas-se, dans tes lour-des tres-ses, Un par-fum sub-til et con-nu;

And just now there rose in my heart A world of en-
Tout à l'heure il m'est re-ve-nu Au coeur de très

trancing caresses, One with that perfume of the past; Of dying flowers t'is the fragrance: Lilac, jasmine, lily and rose, That, adrift in the olden paths, Gentle

lentes caresses De ce parfum et connu; deur des fleurs mourantes: Roses, lilas, lys et jasmin, Que, parmi les anciens chemins, Apporcher C'était l'o-

zeph - yrs have gath - ered and scat - ter O - ver the
taient les bri - ses er - ran - tes Sur ces li -

li - - lac, jas - mine and rose.
las et ces jas - mins.

MADRIGAL
(MADRIGAL)
DANS LE STYLE ANCIEN
(In the old manner)

à Madame Brunet-Lafleur

ROBERT de BONNIÈRES
Translated by Isabella G. Parker

(Composed in 1871-'73)
(Original Key)

VINCENT D'INDY, Op. 4
(1852-)

Where can you find more charming face or fairer, A snowier neck, where soft hair silken lies?— Where was there ever form of beauty rarer Than hath my lady of

Qui jamais fut de plus charmant visage, De col plus blanc, de cheveux plus soyeux;— Qui jamais fut de plus gentil corsage. Qui jamais fut que ma

Copyright MCMIV by Oliver Ditson Company

59

love - li - est eyes?
Dame aux doux yeux!

espress.

a tempo

Where can you find lips ____ more sweet, ev - er smil - ing, Un - to whose
Qui ja - mais eut lè - - vres plus sou - ri - an - tes, Qui sou - ri -

a tempo

p e molto legato
(et très-lié)

(a

smil - ing the fond heart re - plies, ____ Or breast more chaste, 'neath
ant ren - dit coeur plus joy - eux, Plus cha - ste sein sous

molto sostenuto
(très-soutenu)

a)

ML-549-4

veil of gauze be - guil - ing, Than hath my la - dy of love - li - est
guim - pes trans - pa - ren - tes, Qui ja - mais eut que ma Dame aux doux

eyes! Where is a voice of
yeux! Qui ja - mais eut voix

sempre legato ed espress.
(toujours très-lié et expressif)

mu - sic more en - tranc - ing, Or teeth whose white - ness
d'un plus doux en - ten - dre, Mi - gnon - nes dents qui

e'en the pearl out-vies;— Where from a soul more
bouche em-per-lent mieux;— Qui ja-mais fut de

ten-der-ness is glanc-ing Than hath my la-dy of
re-gar-der si ten-dre, Qui ja-mais fut que ma

Molto lento e sempre rall.
(Très-lent et en retenant toujours)

love-li-est eyes, Of love-li-est eyes!—
Dame aux doux yeux, Ma Dame aux doux yeux!—

A SEA SONG
(LIED MARITIME)

(Original Key)

(Composed in 1896)

VINCENT D'INDY
Translated by Isabella G. Parker

VINCENT D'INDY
(1852 —)

à X

Lento moderato (♩=76)
(Modérement lent)

A - far in the o - cean sink - eth the sun,
Au loin, dans la mer, s'é - teint le so - leil,

And the sea is tran - quil and tide - less; The
et la mer est calme et sans ri - de; le

waves, ripp - ling soft - ly, si - lent - ly spread,__ And ca -
flot di - a - pré s'é - ta - le sans bruit,__ ca - res -

Copyright MCMIV by Oliver Ditson Company

ress the strand — as it dark-ens; Thine eyes, thy faith-less eyes are closed, — And my heart is at rest, is calm like the sea.

sant la grève — as-som-bri-e; Tes yeux, tes traî-tres yeux sont clos, — et mon coeur est tran-quil-le com-me la mer.

Più animato (♩=112)
(Plus animé)

... far on the sea, the storm com-eth on, And the
loin, sur la mer, l'o- rage est le- vé, et la

65

o - - cean wild - - ly is
mer s'e - meut et bouil -

rag - - ing; The
lon - - ne; le

waves to the skies mount
flot, jus - qu'aux cieux, s'e -

poco più f

proud - ly a - loft, Then
ri - ge su - perbe, et

ML-550-6

falls t'ward tu - mul - tu - ous a -
croule en hur - lant vers les a -

molto rit.
(très retenu)

byss - - es. Thine
bî - - mes. Tes

poco meno mosso (♩=104)
(un peu moins animé)

eyes, thy faith - less eyes, so sweet, Deep with -
yeux, tes traî - tres yeux si doux me re -

in my in-most soul are gaz - - ing And my
gar - - dent jus-qu'au fond de l'â - - me, et mon

heart in its pain,___ my heart in its joy, With
coeur tor-tu - ré,___ mon coeur bien-heu - reux s'ex -

rap - ture as - cends, then breaks
alte et se bri - se com -

like the sea!
me la mer!

à Madame Julie Lalo

THE CAPTIVE
(L'ESCLAVE)

(Composed about 1872)

THÉOPHILE GAUTIER (1811-1872)
Translated by Nathan Haskell Dole

EDOUARD LALO
(1823-1892)

Andante non troppo

A cap-tive ____ and for-got-ten, ill-fat-ed, I dream ____ of my lov-er of yore, ____ Of days no more! ____

Cap-ti-ve ____ et peut-être ou-bli-é-e, Je songe ____ à mes jeu-nes a-mours, ____ À mes beaux jours! ____

una corda
(sourdine)

Copyright MDCCCXCIX by Oliver Ditson Company

ML-551-3

Of days no more!
À mes beaux jours!

And up thro' my one window grat - ed, I can fol - low the
Et par la fe - nê - tre gril - lé - e Je re - gar - de l'oi-

birds that fly A-cross the sky.
seau joy - eux Fen-dant les cieux!

without taking breath
(sans respirer)

O love - ly bird, hope of the mor - row,
Au - près de lui, belle es - pé - ran - ce,

Bear me far on thy wings like a dove's! If still he loves!
Por - te - moi sur tes ai - les d'or, S'il m'aime en - cor!

If still he loves!
S'il m'aime en - cor!

And then as a balm for my sor - row, My soul to-day up
Et pour en - dor - mir ma souf - fran - ce Sus - pens mon â - me

on his breast Flow'r-like shall rest!
Sur son coeur Comme u - ne fleur!

COUNTESS, IN THY DANCING
(VOUS DANSEZ, MARQUISE)
GAVOTTE DES MATHURINS

EUGENE BAZOT
Translated by Nathan Haskell Dole

GASTON LEMAIRE
(1854-   )

Count-ess, in thy danc-ing Light thou art as air! With thy grace en-tranc-ing Flowers can not com-pare. Birds that pierce the a-zure Look with en-vious eye,

Vous dan-sez, mar-quise, D'un pied si lé-ger Qu'en pas-sant, la bri-se Ne peut moins pe-ser, La fleur est sans grâ-ce, Certe, au-près de vous,

Copyright MCMI by Oliver Ditson Company

ML-552-6

While in per-fect meas-ure Swift thy young feet fly. Per-fume sub-tly
L'oi - seau, dans l'es - .pa - ce De vous est ja - loux. Un par-fum qui

wreath - ing, Am - ber-gris and rose, From thy rai - ment breath-ing,
gri - se Fait d'am-bre et d'i - ris, Vient de vous, mar - qui - se,

Where thou go - est goes. And the fleck of beau - ty On thy lil - y
À mon coeur é - pris. La mou - che que po - se Mar - ton cha - que

brow Chains my love and du - ty, Seals my dear - est vow.
jour Sur vo - tre front ro - se, ap - pel - le l'a - mour.

ML-552-6

73

Thou'st a roy-àl pile of ra-ven tress-es Thy white hand ca-ress-es,
Sur vos noirs che-veux la pou-dre jet-te, Mar-qui-se co-quet-te,

Frost-ed by thine art! Bright the brown eyes smile And light-ly
Un fri-mas trem-blant Et de vos grands yeux Jail-lit la

cap-ture In a net of rap-ture Thy lov-er's heart.
flam-me Qui pé-nè-tre l'â-me De votre a-mant.

E'en as Co-lin to Ja-votte said, glanc-ing In her eyes as they were danc-ing "I'm
Comme en dan-sant tous deux la ga-vot-te, Co-lin di-sait à Ja-vot-te: "À

thine, Thou'rt mine?" So when we two trip the meas-ure
toi Ma foi!" Ain-si quand nous al-lons en ca-

sprightly Hear my heart re-peat-ing lightly One word
den-ce Tout au plai-sir de la dan-se, Mon coeur,

Thou'st heard. And my eyes be-tray my ex-ul-ta-tion By their
Sans peur, Ré-pè-te que c'est vous que j'a-do-re Mon re-

ea-ger a-dor-a-tion: They see But thee!
gard le dit en-co-re Si doux Pour vous!

Count-ess, close thy fan that hides thy blush - es! How I love those peach-down flush-es! Those
Fer-mez votre é - ven-tail qui m'em - pê - che De voir vo - tre teint de pê - che, Vos

eyes I prize! Since I love thee mad - ly, Since my heart's on
yeux Si bleus. Et quand je vous ai - me D'u - ne folle ar -

fire, Thee I'd die for glad - ly — Crown my heart's de - sire! Thou art beau-ty's
deur D'un bon-heur su - prê - me Rem - plis - sez mon coeur: Vous ê - tes trop

jew - el, I am all de - spair; Count-ess, be not cru - el; Hear the
bel - le, Moi trop mal - heu - reux, Soy - ez moins cru - el - le, Com - blez

vows I swear! See the dance so state-ly; La-dy, take my hand
tous mes voeux! Voy-ez comme on dan-se La main dans la main,

And we'll march se-date-ly, Join-ing Hy-men's band! Count-ess, in thy
Al-lons en ca-den-ce Jus-qu'au doux hy-men... Vous dan-sez, mar-

danc-ing Light thou art as air! With thy grace en-tranc-ing, Flow'rs can
qui-se, D'un pied si lé-ger Qu'en pas-sant la bri-se Ne peut

not com-pare!
moins pe-ser.

più mosso
(plus vive)

à Madame C. Salla-Uhring

THE NILE
(LE NIL)

(Original Key)

D'ARMAND RENAUD
Translated by Isabella G. Parker

XAVIER LEROUX
(1863-)

The sol - emn Nile_____ with its pale wa - ters
Les eaux du Nil_____ tou - tes pâ - les, s'é -

flow - - ing_____
cou - - lent,_____

Copyright MCMIV by Oliver Ditson Company

Un- der the stars of sum- mer
Sous les é- toi- les de la

night. Ah!
nuit, Ah!

Ah!
Ah!

A - long the
Des sphinx, aux

shore_____ sphinx-es dim-ly are show_____ing.
bords,_____ sur deux rangs se dé-rou_____lent,

Ah!_____
Ah!_____

Ah!_____
Ah!_____

mf
pp
In mid -
Au mi -
mf
p
Ped.
stream floats our bark so light.
lieu, no - tre bar - que fuit
ppp
poco più lento (un peu plus lent)
My dear - est one, lean - ing there on the
Le bien - ai - mé, s'ac - cou - dant sur la
pp
prow, Turns his eyes of
proue, lais - se er - rer sur
p
cresc.
pp
mf

love _____ on me now: _____ I _____ with my head re-
moi _____ son œil doux, _____ Moi, ren-ver-sant la

clin-ing _____ in the breeze, My gold-en hair _____ up-on his
tê - te, _____ je se-coue Mes che-veux d'or _____ sur ses ge-

knees. _____ From their vast plain do _____ the
noux. _____ Et les grands sphinx, dans la

sphinx - es be-hold _____ Our frag-ile boat now
plai - ne in-fi-nie, _____ Nous _____ re-gar-dant pas-

pass - ing near. With min-gled voice____ they__ soft mu-sic un - fold,____ They__ soft mu-sic un-fold,____ That through__ love's en - chant - ment__ we

ser__ près d'eux, Con - fu - sé - ment____ ver - sent une har - mo - nie,____ Ver - sent une har - mo - nie____ Qui tombe__ en a - mour sur___ nous

hear.
deux.

PROVENCE SONG
(CHANT PROVENÇAL)

MICHEL CARRÉ (1819-1872)
Translated by Isabella G. Parker

JULES MASSENET
(1842-   )

Andantino sostenuto

Mi-rel-la doth not know she hold-eth Such a charm in her win-some grace! She like a love-ly bud un-fold-eth When smiled up-on by sum-mer's face! Who know-eth not Mi-rel-la, los-eth Heav'n's

Mi-reil-le ne sait pas en-co-re Le doux char-me de sa beau-té! C'est u-ne fleur qui vient dé-clo-re Dans un sou-ri-re de l'é-té! À qui ne con-naît pas Mi-reil-le, Dieu

Copyright MCMIV by Oliver Ditson Company

ML-554-4

choic-est gift of treas-ure rare! Her beau-ty a ri-val re-
ca-che son plus cher tré-sor! Sa grâ-ce à nulle au-tre pa-

fus-eth With gold-en dress be-yond com-pare!
reil-le La pa-re mieux qu'un man-teau d'or!

Mi-rel-la doth not know she hold-eth Such a charm in her win-some
Mi-reil-le ne sait pas en-co-re Le doux char-me de sa beau-

grace!
té!

She like a love-ly bud un-
C'est u-ne fleur qui vient d'é-

fold - eth When smiled up - on by sum - mer's face!
clo - re Dans un sou - ri - re de l'é - té!

poco rit.

a tempo

Naught dis-turb-eth the dream of pleas - ure In her heart, pure and
Rien ne trou - ble le chas - te rê - ve De son cœur in - no-

dolce   *mf cresc.*

free from guile. Smil - ing, she be-holds morn - ing's treas - ure, The
cent et pur. El - le rit au jour qui se lè - ve, Le

day re - plies with a smile. Mi - rel - la doth not know she
jour lui sou - rit dans l'a - zur. Mi - reil - le ne sait pas en -

hold-eth Such a charm in her win-some grace! She like a love-ly bud un-fold-eth When smiled up-on by sum-mer's face, When smiled up-on by sum-mer's face!

co-re Le doux char-me de sa beau-té! C'est u-ne fleur qui vient d'é-clo-re Dans un sou-ri-re de l'é-té, Dans un sou-ri-re de l'é-té!

OPEN THY BLUE EYES
(OUVRE TES YEUX BLEUS)

PAUL ROBIQUET
Translated by Arthur Westbrook

(Original Key, F)

JULES MASSENET
(1842-)

Allegro, con molto anima
(Avec assez d'animation)

He *(Lui)*

O - pen thy blue eyes now, my dar - - ling, 'Tis dawn of day; On the leaf - y bough trills the star - - ling His am'rous lay. Au - ro - ra with the hue of ro - - ses

Ou - vre tes yeux bleus, ma mi - gnon - - ne: Voi - ci le jour. Dé - jà la fau - vet - te fre - don - - ne Un chant d'a - mour. L'au - rore é - pa - nou - it la ro - - se.

Copyright MCMIV by Oliver Ditson Company

Doth tinge the skies; The lovely marguerite uncloses; My love, arise! My love, arise!

Viens a-vec moi Cueil-lir la marguerite éclose. Réveille-toi! Réveille-toi!

O-pen thy blue eyes now, my dar - - - ling,
Ou - vre tes yeux bleus, ma mi - gnon - - - ne;

'Tis dawn of day! Why re-gard na-ture's face, which
Voi - ci le jour! A quoi bon con - tem - pler la

glow - eth in ra - diance bright? No
ter - re Et sa beau - té? L'a -

sum - mer day such joy be - stow - - eth As love's de-
mour est un plus doux mys - tè - - re Qu'un jour d'é -

light._____ From my breast sweet-est songs are
té;_____ C'est en moi que l'oi- seau mo-

soar - - ing With con- qu'ring art,_____
dule_____ Un chant vain - queur,_____

And the rays of sun- light are pour - - ing
Et le grand so- leil qui nous brû - - le

From out my heart!_____
Est dans mon coeur!_____

HOW BRIEF IS THE HOUR
(QUE L'HEURE EST DONC BRÈVE)

ARMAND SILVESTRE (1839-1901)
Translated by Isabella G. Parker

JULES MASSENET
(1842-)

The hour swift is fly-ing Of Love's brief de-light! 'Tis gone from our sight, And dream-like, 'tis dy-ing; Time steals, on-ward fly-ing, Our love-vi-sions bright. The hour swift is fly-ing, Of Love's brief de-light!

Que l'heure est donc brè-ve, Qu'on passe en ai-mant! C'est moins qu'un mo-ment, Un peu plus qu'un rê-ve. Le temps nous en-lè-ve Notre en-chan-te-ment. Que l'heure est donc brè-ve, Qu'on passe en ai-mant!

Love's de-light! Be-neath the wave's flow The sands soft are sigh-ing; "Dost love me, or no?" Is it but a dream, That, dream-like is dy-ing? The hour swift is fly-ing, Of Love's brief de-light! Love's de-light!

En ai-mant! Sous le flot dor-mant Sou-pi-rait la grè-ve; M'ai-mas-tu vrai-ment? Fût-ce seu-le-ment Un peu plus qu'un rê-ve? Que l'heure est donc brè-ve, Qu'on passe en ai-mant! En ai-mant!

94

à Madame Galli-Marié

HAVANAISE
(LA ISLENA — L'ISOLANA)

(*Original Key, C*)

From the Spanish
English version by Isabella G. Parker

E. PALADILHE
(1844-)

When the plane-trees are gloom-ing With high arch-es green, Where the vines bright-ly bloom-ing Sus-pend-ed are seen; There my light ham-mock sway-ing Moves soft to and

Au mi- lieu des pla- ta- nes Aux lar- ges fron- tons, Où la fleur des li- a- nes Sus- pend ses fes- tons; Mon ha- mac se ba- lan- ce, Ber- çant mol- le-

Copyright MCMIV by Oliver Ditson Company

M L - 557 - 10

fro Dream-y thoughts i-dly stray-ing Like winds come and go, Thus half a-
ment Ma rê-veuse in-do-len-ce, Au souf-fle du vent, Dans un de-

sleep in shade____ From the burn-ing sun's glare; I____ drink
mi som-meil____ À l'a-bri du so-leil Je____ m'en-

rich-est per-fume____ of tu-lip red and rare, Far in the
i-vre aux par-fums____ du tu-li-pier ver-meil Dans les nu-

cloud-lets blue____ Where my eyes are glan-cing, I____ be__
a-ges bleus____ Si je plon-ge les yeux En____ un____

hold heav'n un-closed In dreams en-tran - cing!
son - ge en-chan - teur Je vois s'ou - vrir les cieux!

Ev - er gay and free,
Li - bre et sans sou - ci

Thus to be Dream-ing all the mer - ry day,
Vi - vre ain-si En rê - vant le long du jour

Vows will we be-guile With a smile, Waft-ing lov-ers' sighs a-way. Love if we re-ceive, Nev-er give While the heart in safe-ty is, Is it not to you, Tell me true, All the se-cret of bliss? Where the

Ri - re des ser - ments Des ga - lants Et de leurs sou - pirs d'a - mour Se lais - ser ai - mer Et char - mer Sans ja - mais don - ner son coeur N'est - ce pas, ma foi Di - tes - moi, Le se - cret du bon - heur? Au mi -

plane-trees are gloom-ing With bright arch-es green, Where the
lieu des pla - ta - nes Aux lar - ges fron - tons, Où la

vines, bright-ly bloom-ing, Sus-pend-ed are seen; There my
fleur des li - a - nes Sus-pend ses fes - tons; Mon ha-

light ham-mock sway-ing, Moves soft to and fro, Dream-y
mac se ba - lan - ce, Ber-çant mol - le - ment Ma rê -

thoughts, i-dly stray-ing, Like winds come and go. Thus half a-
veuse in - do - len - ce, Au souf - fle du vent Dans un de -

When the eve-ning star shines a-far, Then on bal-co-ny a-bove, Soft-est words to hear Of lov-er dear
Quand l'é-toi-le luit Dans la nuit S'ac-cou-der sur son bal-con, É-cou-ter les voeux D'un a-mou-reux

Mur - mur - ing his song of love, Then to bid him weep
Qui mur - mu - re sa chan - son. Le lais - ser pleu - rer

With sighs so deep, While your face all smil - ing
Et sou - pi - rer En ri - ant de son ar -

is, Is it not to you, Tell me true,
deur, N'est - ce pas ma foi, Di - tes moi,

All the se - cret of bliss? Where the
Le se - cret du bon - heur? Au mi -

plane-trees are gloom-ing With high arch-es green, Where the
lieu des pla - ta - nes Au lar - ges fron - tons, Où la

a tempo
pp
con Pedale

vines bright-ly bloom-ing, Sus-pend-ed are seen, There my
fleur des li - a - nes Sus - pend ses fes - tons Mon ha -

light ham-mock sway-ing, Moves soft to and fro, Dream-y
mac se ba - lan - ce Ber - cant mol - le - ment, Ma rê -

thoughts, i-dly stray-ing, Like winds come and go. Thus, half a-
veuse in - do - len - ce, Au souf - fle du vent Dans un dé -

f

103

sleep in shade___ From the burn-ing sun's glare, I drink
mi som-meil___ À l'a-bri du so-leil Je m'en-

rich-est___ per-fume___ of tu-lip red and rare. Far in the
i-vre aux par-fums___ du tu-li-pier ver-meil, Dans les nu-

cloud-lets blue___ Where my eyes are glan-cing, I be-
a-ges bleus___ Si je plon-ge les yeux En un___

hold heav'n un-closed in___ dreams en - tran - cing!___
son - ge en chan - teur___ Je___ vois s'ou - vrir les cieux!

GOOD MORNING, CLAIRE!
(BONJOUR, SUZON!)
(AUBADE)

ALFRED DE MUSSET (1810-1857)
Translated by Nathan Haskell Dole

ÉMILE PESSARD
(1843-   )

Good morn-ing, Claire, good morn-ing, Claire, my wood-land flow'r! And art thou still, and art thou still our pret-tiest maid-en? From I-ta-lia's shores I am come this hour, With stores of

Bon-jour, Su-zon! Bon-jour, Su-zon! ma fleur des bois! Es-tu tou-jours, es-tu tou-jours la plus jo-li-e? Je re-viens, tel que tu me vois, D'un grand voy-

Copyright MCMIV by Oliver Ditson Company

ML-558-5

bright-est memories laden. Thro' Para-
a geen I - ta - li - e. Du pa - ra-

dise I wan-dered long, I fash-ioned rhymes, Love was my
dis j'ai fait le tour, J'ai fait des vers, chan - té l'a -

song! What's that to thee, dear, what to thee,
mour; Mais que t'im - por - te, que t'im - por -

dear! I wan - der be-fore thy door, my fair. Look forth and
te! Je pas - se de - vant ta mai - son; Ou - vre ta

see, dear! Look forth and see, dear! I wander before thy door, my fair! Good morning, Claire! Good morning, Claire! When we parted the flow'rs were in their prime: Did not thy heart new joy dis-

porte, ouvre ta porte! Je passe devant ta maison! Bonjour, Suzon! Bonjour, Suzon! Je t'ai vue au temps des lilas Ton cœur joyeux venait d'é-

cov-er! And yet thou saidst: "'Tis not the time, 'tis not the
clo-re, Et tu di-sais: "Je ne veux pas, je ne veux

time to choose a lov-er." While I was
pas Qu'on m'ai-me en-co-re." Qu'as-tu fait

gone what's been thy fate? Who goes too soon re-turns too
de-puis mon dé-part? Qui part trop tôt re-vient trop

regretfully

carelessly

late; What's that to me, dear, what to me,
tard; Mais que m'im-por-te, que m'im-por -

108

SERENADE
(SÉRÉNADE)

(Original Key, D)

EUGÈNE ADENIS
Translated by Isabella G. Parker

GABRIEL PIERNÉ, Op. 7
(1863 –   )

Up-on the breast of night _____ A star is gleam-ing bright. _____
Au sein des nuits tout dort, _____ L'é-toi-le brille en-cor, _____

The wind is soft be-low, _____ Where li-lacs blow; _____
Le vent se tait là-bas, _____ Dans les li-las. _____

Be-neath the fo-liage blest _____ The bird has
Sous le feuil-lage a-mi, _____ L'oi-seau s'est

Copyright MCMIV by Oliver Ditson Company

ML-559-6

gone to rest. Come, the for-est gloom Sheds rich per-fume; Up-on the
en - dor - mi. Viens, les bois char - més Sont em - bau - més; Au sein des

breast of night, Yes, A star is gleam-ing bright. Come, O thou my
nuits tout dort. Oui, l'é - toi - le brille en - cor, Viens, ô mon a -

love, for I am thine. Be on-ly mine! Let our sweet musings
mour, je t'ap - par - tiens, Sois toute à moi! Lais - sons er - rer nos

wan-der Through paths of per-fume and of song.
â - mes Sur les par - fums et les chan - sons.

Let our love to dreams be long.
Ai - mons - nous, ai - mons, rê - vons.

But a - las! are my la - bors in vain?
Mais hé - las! est-ce en vain que ma voix

No ech - o re - sponds yet a - gain.
Fait gé - mir l'é - cho de ces bois?

Come, soft is the air. Night is so fair, Ah! come! Ah! come!
Viens, l'air est si doux Au - tour de nous, Ah! viens! Ah! viens!

Ah! _____

Up-on the breast of night _____
Au sein des nuits tout dort,

A star is gleam-ing bright. _____ The wind is
L'é - toi - le brille en - cor, *Le vent se*

soft be - low, _____ Where li - lacs grow. _____
tait là - bas, *Dans les li - las.*

Be-neath the fo - liage blest _____
Sous le feuil - lage a - mi,

The bird hath gone to rest. Come, the for-est gloom Sheds rich per-fume; Up-on the breast of night, Yes, A star is gleam-ing bright. Come, O thou my love, For I am thine. Be on-ly mine!

L'oi-seau s'est en-dor-mi. Viens, les bois char-més Sont em-bau-més; Au sein des nuits tout dort. Oui, l'é-toi-lé brille en-cor, Viens, ô mon a-mour, je t'ap-par-tiens, Sois toute à moi!

Let our sweet mus-ings wan-der Through paths of per-fume and of song;
While our fond hearts grow fond-er
Time fly-eth, and we are gone, O Love! O Love!

*Lais - sons er - rer nos â - mes Sur les par - fums et les chan - sons,
Le temps où nous ai - mâ - mes
S'en - vo - le et nous pas - sons. Ai - mons! Ai - mons!*

à Mademoiselle Marguerite Lavigne

LULLABY
(BERCEUSE)

(*Original Key, D*)

HIPPOLYTE LUCAS
Translated by Alexander Blaess

J. GUY ROPARTZ
(1864 -

Now, ye lit-tle folk, Let all noise a-bate and peace dwell in the house! In pray'r kneel in your ti-ny beds, Be sure to mind with bet-ter

O pe-tits en-fants, voi-ci l'heure Où tout bruit cesse en la de-meure. Pri-ez en vo-tre lit cou-chés, Pro-met-tez bien d'ê-tre plus

Copyright MCMIV by Oliver Ditson Company

grace; All out-bursts of pas-sion and wrath
sa - ges, Les tré - pi - gne - ments et les ra - ges

Blot your soul with the stain of sin!
Sont de gros, de très - gros pé - chés!

Hush! hush! go to sleep; You will see an an-gel
Do - do, dou - ce - ment, Vous ver - rez un ange en dor -

fair. You will see the man-ger In
mant. Vous ver - rez la crèche el - le

which our gen-tle Sa-viour, the Son of God, was born as a frail help-less babe, Sur-round-ed by shep-herds a-dor-ing, and three Kings, come from farth-est East, Their price-less treas-ures be-

même Où l'en-fant Dieu, Sau-veur su-prême, Na-quit tout ché-tif et souf-frant; Et puis, u-nis-sant leurs hom-ma-ges, Les ber-gers près des trois Rois Ma-ges, A-vec les oi-seaux l'a-do-

stow - ing. Hush! hush! go to sleep,
rant. Do - do, dou - ce - ment

Tempo I

You will see an an - gel fair.
Vous ver - rez un ange en dor - mant.

poco più lento
(un peu plus lent)

Not on - ly to your moth - er dear You cause sad-ness and bit - ter tears,
Non seu - le - ment, à vo - tre mè - re Vous cau - sez u - ne peine a - mè - re

You that were born to be her joy: But the gen - tle
Vous, nés pour fai - re son bon - heur; Mais au ciel Jé -

Je - sus is griev-ed by your faults; for to his
sus se cha - gri - ne cha - que faute a - joute une é -

crown Ev-'ry trans-gres-sion adds a thorn.
pine À la cou - ron - ne du Sei - gneur.

Hush! hush! go to sleep; You will see an an - gel
Do - do, dou - ce - ment, Vous ver - rez un ange en dor -

poco rit.

fair.
mant.

Tempo I

WHY WITH YOUR LOVELY PRESENCE HAUNT ME
(SI VOUS N'AVEZ RIEN À ME DIRE)
ROMANCE

To Miss Fanny Reed

VICTOR HUGO (1802-1885)
Translated by Arthur Westbrook

Baroness WILLY de ROTHSCHILD

Why with your love-ly pres-ence haunt me, If there is naught that you would tell? Your witch-ing smile is but to taunt me, Yet e'en a king might fear its spell. Your witch-ing smile is but to taunt me, Yet e'en a king might fear its spell. Why with your love-ly

Si vous n'a-vez rien à me di-re, Pour-quoi ve-nir au-près de moi? Pour-quoi me fai-re ce sou-ri-re Qui tour-ne-rait la tête au roi. Si vous n'a-vez rien à me di-re Pour-quoi ve-nir au-près de moi? Si vous n'a-vez rien

Copyright MCMIV by Oliver Ditson Company

ML-561-4

pres - ence haunt me, If there is naught that you would tell?
à me di - re Pour - quoi ve - nir au - près de moi?

If you would teach me
Si vous n'a - vez rien

no wise sto - ry, Why warm - ly press my hand, I pray?
à m'ap - pren - dre, Pour - quoi me pres - sez - vous la main?

While ten - der dreams of heav'n - ly glo - ry En - chant your spir - it as you stray?
Sur le rêve an - gé - lique et tendre Au - quel vous son - gez en che - min?

122

While ten-der dreams of heav'n-ly glo-ry, En-chant your spir-it as you stray!
Si vous n'a-vez rien à m'ap-pren-dre, Pour-quoi me pres-sez-vous la main,

If you would teach me no wise sto-ry, Why warm-ly press my hand, I
Si vous n'a-vez rien à m'ap-pren-dre Pour-quoi me pres-sez-vous la

pray?
main?

If 'tis your wish that I should leave you, Why pass this way so soon a-gain?
Si vous vou-lez que je m'en ail-le, Pour-quoi pas-sez-vous par i-ci?

ML-561-4

I trem-ble when my eyes per-ceive you;— 'Tis my joy and a-las! my pain.
Lors-que je vous vois, je tres-sail-le:— C'est ma joie et c'est mon sou-ci.

If 'tis your wish that I should leave you Why pass this way so soon a-gain,
Si vous vou-lez que je m'en ail-le Pour-quoi pas-sez vous par i-ci,

If 'tis your wish that I should leave you Why pass this way so soon a-gain?
Si vous vou-lez que je m'en ail-le Pour-quoi pas-sez-vous par i-ci?

124

à Madame Pauline Viardot

THE BELL
(LA CLOCHE)

(Composed in 1856)

(Original Key)

VICTOR HUGO (1802-1885)
Translated by Arthur Westbrook

CAMILLE SAINT-SAËNS
(1835-   )

Lone__ in thy dark old tow'r__ with tur-rets scarred and drear, Whence thy deep voice de-scends on the roofs clus-t'ring near, O bell, high o-ver all,__ 'mid the clouds thou art

Seule__ en ta som-bre tour__ aux fai-tes den-te-lés, D'où ton souf-fle des-cend sur les toits é-bran-lés, Ô clo-che sus-pen-du-e au mi-lieu des nu-

Copyright MCMIV by Oliver Ditson Company

M L-562-6

hung,__ Which so of-ten re-sound to thy clam-or-ous tongue.__
é - es, Par ton vas-te rou-lis si sou-vent re-mu-é -

__ In shad-ow now thou sleep-est, hushed__ is ev'-ry
es, Tu dors en ce mo-ment dans l'ombre,__ et rien ne

sound, In the midst of the dark-ness dwells si-lence pro-
luit Sous ta voû-te pro-fonde où som-meil-le le

found! Oh!_____ when draws near a
bruit! Oh!_____ tan-dis qu'un es-

soul, and, tho' no word is spo- ken,
prit qui jus- qu'à toi s'é- lan- ce,

Soars up to thee on high through si- lence yet un-
Si- len- ci- eux aus- si, con- tem- ple ton si-

bro- ken, Dost not some in- stinct feel—
len- ce, Sens- tu, par cet ins- tinct

Vague- ly bless- ed and dear— Which must ev- er re-
vague et plein de dou- ceur Qui ré- vè- le tou-

veal_ that a sis - ter is near?_ In this
jours_ u - ne sœur à la sœur,_ Qu'à cette

hour of re - pose_ when the twi - light is
heure où s'endort_ la soi - rée ex - pi -

dy - ing, A soul_ is near to thee;
ran - te, Une âme_ est près de toi,

like thee it, too, is cry - ing;
non moins que toi vi - bran - te,

Cry - ing with sol - emn sound to the blue vault on high, And doth mourn in its love e'en as thou in the sky!

Qui bien sou - vent aus - si jette un bruit so - len - nel, Et se plaint dans l'a - mour com - me toi dans le ciel!

And doth mourn in its love e'en as
Et se plaint dans l'amour com - me

thou in the sky,
toi dans le ciel!

in the sky!
dans le ciel!

MOONLIGHT
(CLAIR DE LUNE)

(Original Key)

à Madame Marie Barbier

CATULLE MENDÈS (1841-)
Translated by Isabella G. Parker

CAMILLE SAINT-SAËNS
(1835-)

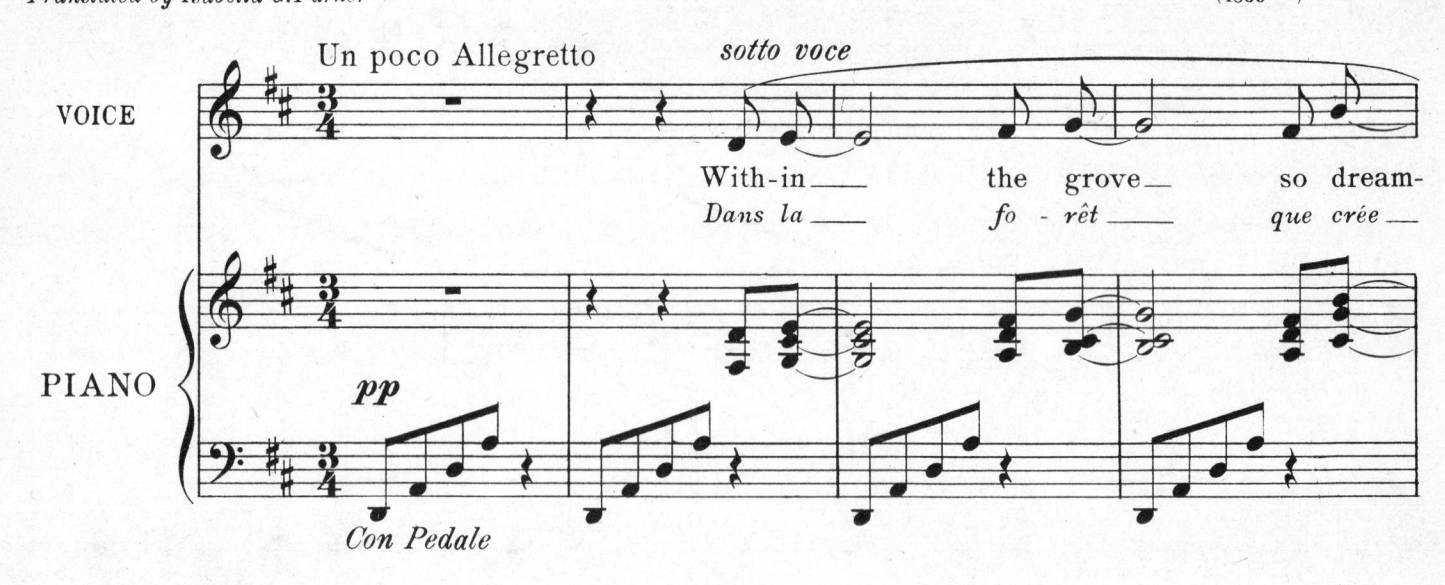

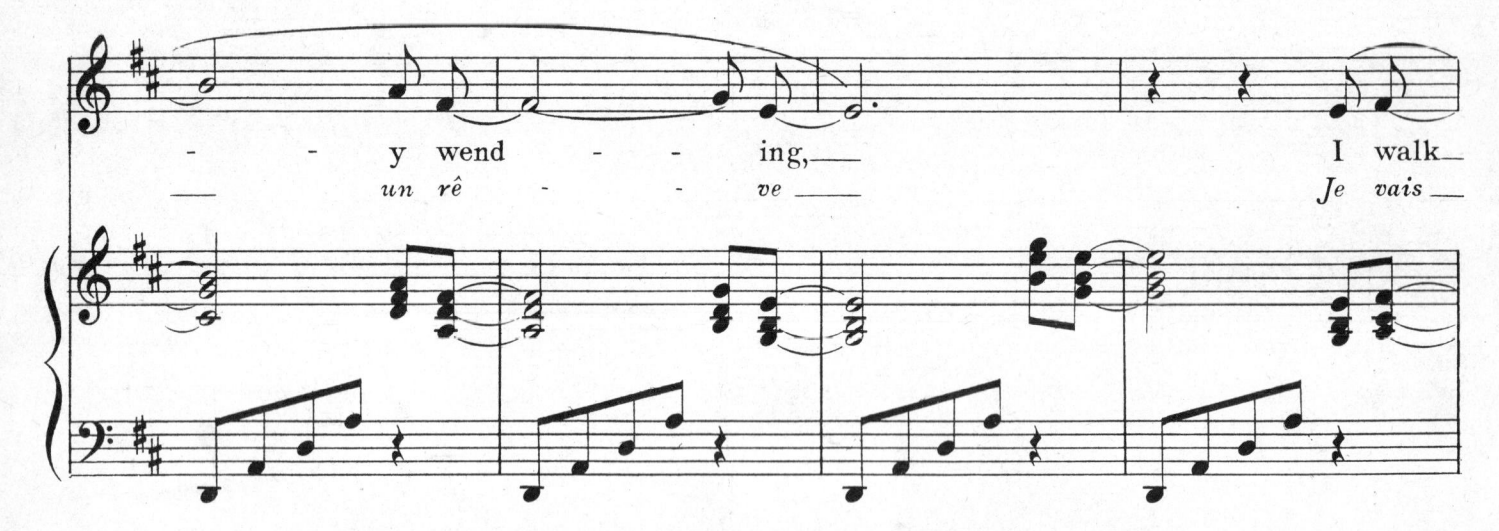

With-in the grove so dream-y wend-ing, I walk at eve the for-est lone.

Dans la fo-rêt que crée un rê-ve Je vais le soir dans la fo-rêt;

Copyright MCMIV by Oliver Ditson Company

Ap - pears ___ thy frail ___ im - age, ___ my own, ___ Be - side me ___ each mo - ment ___ at - tend - - - - ing.

Ta frèle ___ i - ma - - ge m'ap - pa - rait ___ Et che - mine ___ a - vec moi ___ sans trè - - - - ve.

Or is it not thy film - y veil, ___
N'est - ce pas là ton voi - le fin, ___

Like va-por through the dark-ness gleam-ing? Or is it not the moon-light beam-ing? A-cross the pine-tree's shad-ow pale? And these tears that ev - - er are burn - ing— Can they be my

Brouil-lard lé - ger dans la nuit bru - ne? Ou n'est - ce que le clair de lu - ne À tra - vers l'om-bre du sa - pin? Et ces lar - mes, sont - - ce les mien - - nes Que j'en-tends cou -

own tender tears? Or can it
ler doucement? Ou se peut-

be, as it appears, that thou to
il réellement Qu'à mes cô-

me art in tears return
tés, en pleurs, tu vien

ing?
nes?

EVENING
(LE SOIR)

(Published in 1885)
(Original Key)

MICHEL CARRÉ (1819-1872)
Translated by Isabella G. Parker

AMBROISE THOMAS
(1811-1896)

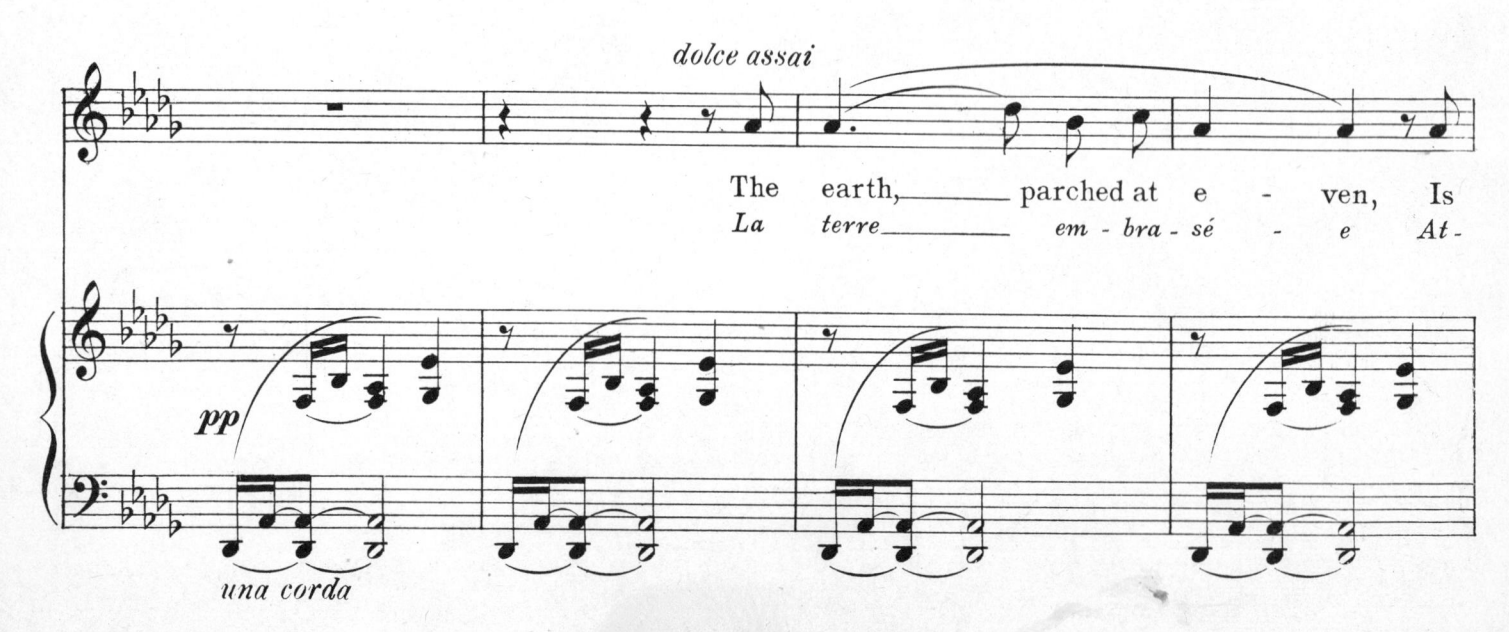

The earth,_____ parched at e - ven, Is
La terre_____ em - bra - sé - e At-

dolce assai

una corda

Copyright MCMIV by Oliver Ditson Company

135

wait - - ing that heav - en The fresh dew may bring.
tend___ la ro - sé - e Qui tom - be des cieux.

Cool - er winds are
La cha - leur s'a-

dim. *pp*

blow - ing, Blest___ re - lief be - stow - ing. The birds sweet-er
pai - se, On___ res - pire à l'ai - se, L'oi-seau chan - te

poco cresc.

sing, The birds___ sweet - er sing.
mieux, L'oi - seau___ chan - te mieux.

dim.
pp
Shad - ows, deep de - scend - - ing, From the trees are
Le feuil - la - ge som - - bre Cou - - vre de son
bend - ing___ Where fond lov - ers meet.
om - bre___ Les a - mants heu - reux
While the star - beams ten - - - der
Et plus d'une é - toi - - le,
pp

137

Thro' their veil of splen - dor Tell love's sto - ry sweet, While star-beams ten - der Tell love's sto - ry sweet, love's sto - ry sweet, love's sto - ry sweet.

À tra - vers son voi - le, Parle aux a - mou - reux, Plus d'une é - toi - le Par - le aux a - mou - reux, aux a - mou - reux, aux a - mou - reux.

ML-564-4

A LOVE SONNET
(SONNET D'AMOUR)

(Original Key, D♭)

A. de SAINEVILLE
Translated by Isabella G. Parker

FRANCIS THOMÉ
(1850 -)

Gold-en the sun-light, beam-ing bright-ly, Gild-eth with lus-tre rich thy hair. I would fain through thy tresses fair Like zeph-yr be float-ing so lightly; And on thy charming neck, where shineth One bright curl wav-ing in the soft air, How would I breathe perfume most rare, That in my soul it-self en-

Sous le so-leil qui les ir-ri-se, En dor-ant leur re-flets soy-eux Je vou-drais dans tes blonds che-veux pas-ser lé-ger com-me la bri-se, Et sur ton cou char-mant où frise U-ne boucle aux plis on-du-leux, En res-pi-rer, vo-lup-tu-eux, L'en-iv-rant par-fum qui me

Copyright MCMIV by Oliver Ditson Company

shrin - eth. Then, if by chance In care-less mood,
gri - se. Comme au ha - sard, sans y pen - ser,

Wouldst thou in-deed ac - count it rude
Se - rait-ce vrai-ment t'of - fen - ser
Should I, as all my soul de-sir-eth,
Si sur tes lè - vres de ce - ri - se

On thy lips, my gen - tle dove, Led by the love thy charm in-spir - eth,
Je met-tais, sa - chant t'a-pai-ser A-vec l'a-mour que tu m'a pri - se,

Pour out my soul, ah, pour out my soul in one kiss of love?
Tou - te ma vi - e, Tou - te ma vi - e en un bai - ser?

THE SIGH
(SOUPIR)

THÉOPHILE GAUTIER (1811-1872)
Translated by Isabella G. Parker

CHARLES WIDOR
(1845-   )

Andantino

From my breast dropt a love-ly flow-ret,__ So bright yet the stream was its grave; A- las! A- las! A- las! I know not how I can re-store it, All wet,__ all cold in the dark

J'ai lais-sé__ de mon sein de nei-ge__ Tom-ber un oeil-let rouge à l'eau; Hé- las! Hé- las! Hé- las! Com-ment, com-ment le re-pren-drai-je Mouil-lé__ par l'on-de du ruis-

wave. I see now the swift wa-ters
seau! Voi - là le cou - rant qui l'en-

bear thee, Blos-som fair with col-ors so bright; Ah,
traî - ne, Bel oeil - let aux vi - ves cou - leurs, Pour-

why must fate thus from me tear thee? My tears are thine, thou dear de-
quoi tom - ber dans la fon - tai - ne Pour t'ar - ro - ser j'a-vais mes

light. My tears are thine my dear de-
pleurs, Pour t'ar - ro - ser j'a - vais mes

light. From my breast dropt a love-ly flow-ret, So
pleurs. J'ai lais-sé de mon sein de nei-ge Tom-

bright, yet was the stream its grave; A - las! A - las! A-
ber un oeil-let rouge à l'eau, Hé las! Hé las! Hé

las! I know not how I can re-store it, All wet, all cold in the dark
las! Com-ment, com-ment le re-pren-drai-je Mouil-lé par l'on - de du ruis-

wave. A - las! A - las!
seau, Hé - las! Hé - las!